New York State Notary Public Study Guide and Exam Prep 2023-2024

MOST COMPREHENSIVE AND UP-TO-DATE GUIDE WITH 6 PRACTICE TESTS!

Lawrence R. Bentley

&

Morris Test PC

Lost River
Publishing House

COVER DESIGN

JENNIFER LAWRENCE

FIRST EDITION

Contents

Introduction

Becoming a notary can be either a career choice or a side job to help you pay some extra bills. No matter what reason you have for becoming a notary, you are going to need to go through several steps to become a notary. In most states, it is a process of paying fees and filling out applications. However, there are some states where you have to take educational courses and pass an exam. In this book, we are first going to briefly look at the job of a notary and what it entails. Then we're going to help you prepare for the notary exam by giving you some practice tests.

Part 1: General Notary Exam Prep

What is a Notary

A notary is an official who is appointed by the state government to serve the public as an impartial witness when it comes to completing a variety of official fraud-deterrent acts linked to signing important documents. The official acts are referred to as notarizations or notarial acts. Notaries are commissioned publicly as "ministerial" officials, which means they need to follow written rules without significant personal discretion.

The duty of a notary is to screen those who are signing important documents to ensure their true identity, their willingness to sign without intimidation or duress and their awareness of the transaction or document. Some notarizations will also require the notary to put the signer under oath, declaration under penalty of perjury that the information in the document is true and correct. Some documents that typically require a notary include property deeds, wills and powers of attorney.

The foundation of the notary's public trust is impartiality. A notary is duty-bound not to act in situations if they have a personal interest. The public trust that the notary's screening tasks aren't corrupted by self-interest. Impartiality also dictates that a notary won't refuse to serve someone based on race, nationality, religion, politics, sexual orientation or status.

Since the notary is an official representative of the state, they will certify the proper execution of many life-changing documents related to private citizens. Whether these documents are real estate, grant powers of attorney, establish a prenuptial agreement or perform other activities related to the functioning of civil society.

Notaries and the notarization process is responsible for deterring fraud and establishing that individuals know the document they are signing and are a willing participant in the transaction.

A notary will often ask to see a current ID with a photo, physical description and signature. This is often a driver's license or passport. This will help establish a person's identity before signing a document.

A notary in the United States is different from those in other countries. In the United States, a notary is not an attorney, judge or other high-ranking officials. The biggest confusion comes from Notario Publico in other countries, which can make it confusing for immigrants. For this reason, notaries in the United States need to be very clear about what they can and cannot do.

Those who are interested can become a notary in their home state by meeting eligibility requirements and following the necessary steps for the commissioning process. Each state has its own process, but in general, you will fill out an application and pay a state application fee. In some states, you'll also need to take a training course or pass an exam.

Before we look more at the process of becoming a notary, let's take a moment to look more at the notarization process.

What is Notarization

Notarization is a fraud-deterrent process that assures a document is authentic and trustworthy, and all parties in the transaction are aware. The notary public that performs the process uses a three-part system: vetting, certifying and record-keeping. Notarizations are often referred to as "notarial acts." The notary public is a duly appointed and impartial individual who assures that a document is authentic with a genuine signature done without duress or intimidation to ensure the terms of the document can be in full effect. The main value of notarization is the impartial screening of the signer when it comes to identity, willingness and awareness. The notary is essentially protecting the personal rights and property of people from forgers, identity thieves and others looking to exploit vulnerable individuals. Let's take a moment to consider the different notarial acts.

Acknowledgments

These are often performed on documents that control or convey ownership of valuable assets. This would include documents such as property deeds, powers of attorney and trusts. For these documents, the signer needs to appear in person and be positively identified in order to declare or acknowledge that the signature is their own and that the provisions of the document can take effect just as they are written.

Jurats

This is typically performed on evidentiary documents involved in the operation of the civil and criminal justice system. This would include documents such as affidavits, depositions and interrogatories. For these documents, a signer needs to appear in person and speak aloud an oath or affirmation of the truth of the statements in the document. The person who takes the oath or affirmation can be prosecuted for perjury if they don't remain truthful.

Certified Copies

This is done to confirm a reproduction of an original is true, exact and complete. This would include documents like college degrees, passports and other one-and-only personal papers that can't be copy-certified by a public record office like the bureau of vital statistics. This notarization isn't an authorized notarial act in all states, and in the states where it is allowed, it can only be done with certain types of original documents.

Each state has its own laws when it comes to performing notarial acts. While different, these laws are mostly congruent with most common notarizations.

Parts of a Notarization

The first part of a notarization is the notary's screening of the signer for identity, volition and awareness.

The second part of the process is to enter the key details in the "journal of notarial acts." A chronological journal is considered the best practice, but it isn't required by law. In some states, there is a requirement for document signers to provide a signature and thumbprint in the notary's journal.

The third part is the completion of a "notarial certificate" that states which facts are being certified by the notary. The climax is the affixation of the notary's signature and seal of office to the certificate. The seal is a universally recognized symbol and provides the document weight in legal matters since it is made genuine in view of the court of law.

Now that we know what a notary is and how the process of notarization occurs. Let's take a moment to consider why you should consider becoming a notary.

Why Become a Notary

Millions of people have chosen to become notaries, and it remains a high-demand business. While being a notary may not seem like a big deal, they hold a lot of power in the legal community. Becoming a notary is also a great way to have some side income or improve your resume. Let's consider five of the top reasons why you should consider becoming a notary.

Additional Source of Income

Although appointed by the state and serving as a

public official, notaries charge clients directly and get to keep their revenue. This is why many communities have people who serve as mobile notaries. States often regulate how much a notary charges for individual notarizations, but clients will often need more than one signature notarized. Additional fees can also be charged, such as travel, supplies and other expenses.

Notary Signing Agent Certification

If you want to become a notary to have some additional income, then you should consider becoming a notary signing agent or NSA. An NSA is a certified and trained professional that notarizes loan documents in real estate closings. NSAs are the main link between banks and borrowers in order to complete the loan. These notaries are hired by title companies directly, but their services are done as an independent contractor to ensure the loan documents are signed by the borrower, notarized and returned for processing. This line of work increases the income a person can get from notary work.

Resume and Skill Improvement

A variety of industries use the services of a notary,

including banking, finance, medical, legal, government, insurance and even technology. If you become a notary, then you'll be adding to your skill set and can improve your resume while increasing your employee value. From an employer standpoint, notaries serve two main functions: they can notarize documents for co-workers and bosses or for customers. A lot of employers value an employee with notary skills in order to handle all document authentication needs and provide additional services to customers.

Keep a Flexible Schedule

If you choose to become a notary, you can enjoy the flexibility of setting your own work schedule. A notary is a perfect job for home-based workers and those who want a job that fits their schedule. In addition, most people who need the services of a notary request them after normal business hours, so you can easily arrange a time that works best for you.

Provide a Community Resource

Notaries are known for helping people in need. If you want to give back to your community, then being a notary is a great choice. Often people need the services of a notary but can't afford the cost, such as the elderly, homeless and college students. These people often need powers of attorney, residency affidavits, advanced medical directives, college transcripts and enrollment verifications, to name a few. Notaries often set aside some time to work from community centers, retirement homes and campuses with free or low-cost notarizations. It can even be a way to market your services and network for paying clients.

If any of these situations seem appealing to you, then you should definitely look into becoming a notary. To do so, you need to be aware of the general requirements needed to become a notary. Let's take a moment to consider the general requirements of a notary before we start looking at specifics.

General Notary Requirements

Although the process for becoming a notary varies based on the state you live in, the general requirements and steps for becoming a notary are the following:

• Ensure you can meet all of the qualifications of your state.

• Complete an application and submit it to the appropriate state department.

- Pay any required state filing fee.

- If needed, start training from an approved educational vendor.

- If needed, pass a state-administered exam.

- If needed, complete a background check and fingerprinting.

- Receive a commission certificate from the state.

- If needed, get a surety bond.

- File commission paperwork and bond, if required, with the notary regulating official in your state.

- Buy necessary notary supplies.

Let's look a little closer at the process of notary training. This isn't required in all states, but several states do require notaries to complete training before they can get certified.

Notary Training

Notary training is required in the following states:

- California

- Colorado

- Florida

- Missouri

- Montana

- Nevada

- North Carolina

- Ohio

- Oregon

- Pennsylvania

Delaware requires training and continuing education for electronic notaries only.

Notary training needs to be approved by the state, so as long as you sign up for an approved course, you'll be covering the required basics during training. Although not many states require a notary to be trained, most states will support an individual's voluntary education.

If you want to undergo voluntary education, you should check with the notary regulating agency for your state. This is often the Secretary of State's office. Some community colleges will also provide educational courses. There are also a number of online organizations and vendors who will provide notary education. Most of these courses are going to provide practical information that helps you to learn how to perform your official duties.

Whether online or in the classroom, training courses will often take about three to six hours. However, optional training can fall outside of these parameters. There is also no official standard for the cost of notary training, so the cost can vary based on the provider. Online training is often going to cost less than $100, while classroom training typically costs between $100 and $200.

In addition to training, some states will also require individuals to take an exam in order to become a notary.

Notary Exam

Most states don't require a notary exam in order to get certified. The following states require a notary exam:

- California

- Colorado

- Connecticut

- Hawaii

- Louisiana

- Maine

- Montana

- Nebraska

- New York

- North Carolina

- Ohio

- Oregon

- Utah

Wyoming encourages individuals to take an at-home test but doesn't currently require it.

The notary exam takes about an hour. Some exams may require the submission of fingerprints with the state application at the end of the exam.

Another general requirement to become a notary is to have the appropriate bond and insurance.

Notary Bonds and Insurance

Most states require notaries to have a bond and insurance. In fact, thirty states and the District of Columbia require notaries to have a surety bond. The difference is the amount required by the state. The typical amount ranges from $5,000 to $10,000, but the lowest is $500, and the highest is $25,000. The surety bond helps to protect consumers. Should the notary make a mistake that damages someone, the bond will compensate the injured person up to the amount of the bond. The notary is then required to repay the bond company.

Since state laws aren't written to protect notaries but rather the public, liability insurance isn't required by notaries. This is why states require bonds instead. However, individual notaries can choose to purchase errors and omissions insurance policies since they can protect them from claims related to errors made during a notarization.

The last general requirement to consider is the notary commission. After this, we can start looking at specific state requirements.

Notary Commission

Notaries are both regulated and commissioned at the state level. This is often done through the Secretary of State's Office, but in some states, this can also be done by the county clerk or another governing body.

Depending on the requirements in your state, the process to become a notary can take seven to nine weeks. It can also take longer if the state is processing a lot of renewals. The shortest it can take is four weeks if your state has minimal requirements.

Most states have organizations that can help you with the process of becoming a notary. It can be a good idea to use one of these organizations since there are multiple steps that need to be completed in an appropriate order. In Florida, Illinois, and Texas, you are required to use specific vendors, and you can't apply yourself directly.

In most states, once you are certified, you can notarize documents throughout the state. Some states do have unique rules when it comes to jurisdiction. This can limit where you are allowed to notarize within the state or perform notarizations for citizens that don't live in the state.

You should be able to notarize for anyone with a legitimate and legal request with acceptable identification. The main restriction in some states is limiting staff notaries to business-related documents during business hours when employed by a business.

The typical term for a notary is four years, but it can vary by state. Some states can also have five and ten-year terms.

The reason for the difference in requirements is that notaries are commissioned and overseen by individual states. Since state notary laws are different, the requirements can also vary greatly. For example, in California, most notary laws are in place because of lawsuits and public damage.

Now that we have an understanding of the general requirements to become a notary let's get a little more specific. As we've already shown, most states don't require an exam. It is always a good idea to study the general rules and regulations for all notaries, as this is often the bulk of exam questions. Take a moment to consider some practice questions that can help you with the general rules and regulations for a notary.

What You Should Know

Before you take your notary exam, there are some general things you should know. While only a few states require a notary exam, fewer states actually require you to know things specific to their state. In general, most state exams are only going to ask general questions related to all notaries throughout the United States. For this reason, to help you pass your notary exam, we are going to review some key points and general notary requirements, the basic rules and exceptions, the common fines and penalties, and some key points to remember before taking your exam. Then we'll also go over some general tips to help you have the easiest time taking your notary exam.

Key Point and General Notary Requirements

- Notary commissions are valid for four years.

- Notaries can perform notarial acts anywhere within the boundaries of their state.

- Notaries need to clear a background check by having a Live Scan Fingerprinting done before they receive their commission.

- Certain actions will prevent a notary from being commissioned:

  o Failing to disclose convictions and/or arrests on the application.

  o A felony conviction within the last ten years of probation.

  o A misdemeanor conviction within the last five years of probation completion.

○ Not complying with family and child support obligations.

• Notaries are not allowed to provide legal advice about immigration or other legal matters unless they are a practicing attorney who has passed the state bar.

• Laws require a notary to perform notarizations if a proper request is made.

• Any documents that involve real property and powers of attorney require the notary to obtain a right thumbprint.

• Notarial acts and procedures include the following:

○ Acknowledgements

○ Jurats

○ Signature by Mark

○ Proof of Execution by Subscribing to Witness Certificates

○ Certified Copies of Power of Attorney

○ Certified Copies of the Notary's Journal

• In order for a document to be notarized, it needs to meet three criteria:

○ The document must be complete.

○ The document must contain the signature of the principal.

○ The document must have the correct notarial wording.

• Notarial Acts can only be completed by the notary and not the signer.

• Notarial wording can appear on the document or on a loose-leaf certificate.

• The four-step process for performing a notarization needs to be completed in entirety:

○ Identifying the signer.

○ Completing the journal entry.

○ Signing by the principal/signer and using the right

thumbprint when necessary.

○ Fill out the notarial act/wording.

• The notary's sequential journal and seal/stamp need to be kept under the exclusive and direct control of the notary.

Notary Rules and/or Exceptions

• Signers must be identified through Satisfactory Evidence, which is done through one of three processes:

○ Specific Paper Identification Documents

○ Oath of a Single Credible Witness

○ Oath of Two Credible Witnesses

• The maximum fee a notary can charge is $15, with the following exceptions:

○ Depositions can charge $30, with the administration of oath being $7 and the certificate to the deposition another $7. But never higher than a charge of $44.

- The signer of the document needs to personally appear before the notary in order for their signature to be notarized. With the following exceptions:

  ○ A subscribing witness can be used when a signer has another person prove to the notary that they signed the document.

- Signers need to sign both the document and the notary journal. With the following exceptions:

  ○ A signature by mark can occur when the signer is unable to sign or write their name. The signer should have the document notarized by marking a mark in the presence of two witnesses.

- A notary notarizes signatures, but they don't certify documents. With the following two exceptions:

  ○ Copies of the notary's own journal.

  ○ Copies of a Power of Attorney.

- Notaries have a 30-day rule to reply to the Secretary of State with three exceptions:

○ If their stamp/seal is lost or stolen, then an immediate reply is warranted.

○ If their journal is lost or stolen, then an immediate reply is warranted.

○ If their journal is taken by a peace officer, then a ten-day reply is warranted.

• The notary must use their stamp/seal on all notarized documents, with the exception of Subdivision Maps.

• A notaries seal/stamp can't be surrendered to anyone with the following exceptions:

○ A court/judge can require the surrender of the seal/stamp after a commission is revoked when the notary is convicted of a crime related to Notarial Misconduct, including the false completion of a notarial certificate or a felony. In this instance, two things must be noted.

■ The court/judge forwards the seal to the Secretary of State with a certified copy of the conviction judgment.

■ This is the only time someone is allowed to possess the notary seal since you need to destroy the notary seal when the commission is no longer valid.

• The journal needs to be kept under the notary's exclusive and personal control at all times. No one is allowed access to the information in the journal, with the following exceptions:

○ Members of the public can get a lined item copy of the journal with a written request.

○ Under a court order, the examination and copying of the journal can be done in the notary's presence.

○ An employer can perform a business examination and copying of the journal in the presence of the notary.

Common Fines and Penalties

• A $75,000 fine is applied in the following circumstance:

○ Deed of Trust Fraud. This is the willful fraud and false filings in connection with a Deed of Trust on a Single-Family Residence.

• $10,000 penalties occur in two situations:

○ Identity of the Credible Witness. This is the failure to obtain the satisfactory evidence needed to establish the identity of a single credible witness.

○ Penalty of Perjury/Acknowledgement. This is when someone willfully states as true a material fact and/or falsifies a certificate of acknowledgment.

• $2,500 civil penalties can be applied in two circumstances:

○ Failing to provide a notary journal to a peace office when requested.

○ Failing to obtain the required thumbprint.

• $1,500 violations are willful and intentional violations. They can be the following:

○ Using false or misleading advertising where the notary public represents that they have duties, rights or privileges that they don't possess.

○ Committing any act that involves dishonesty, fraud or notarial misconduct.

o Executing any certificate as a notary that contains a statement known to be false to the notary.

o Violating the prohibition against a notary who holds themselves as an immigration specialist or consultant advertising or

■ Violating the restrictions on charging to assist in completing immigration forms and

■ Violating the restrictions on advertising notarial services in a language other than English

o Translating the words "notary public" into Spanish.

o Failing to fully and faithfully discharge any of the duties or responsibilities required of a notary public.

o Unauthorized manufacturing, duplicating or selling the public seal of a notary.

o Failing to notify the Secretary of State that a public seal is lost, stolen, destroyed or damaged.

• $1,000 fine is applied in the following situation:

○ Unlawful Practice of Law. This is when any person is practicing law but is not an active member of the State Bar.

• $750 violations are not willful oversights that can still be considered violations. This includes the following:

○ Failing to discharge notary duties.

○ Charging more than the prescribed fees stated by notary law.

○ Failing to complete the acknowledgment at the time the signature and seal are affixed to the document.

○ Failing to administer the oath or affirmation as required.

○ Accepting improper identification.

• $500 infraction penalties apply in the following situation:

○ Failing to notify the Secretary of State in two situations

■ Changing a business, mailing or residential address and

■ Changing the name of the notary public.

Along with these penalties, a denial of an application or suspension or revocation of the notary commission can occur. If a person is guilty of a misdemeanor and/or felony, they can also be liable in a civil action for damages.

Key Points to Know

• Certain notarial acts require specific wording. This includes the following:

○ For an acknowledgment, the following specifics are needed:

■ This is the most common form of notarization

■ It must be done in the notary's presence

■ The notary needs to positively identify the signer

■ The signer needs to acknowledge signing the

document

■ Out-of-state acknowledgments are allowed as long as the certification doesn't require the notary to supersede the notarial law in their practicing state

○ For a jurat, the following specifics are needed:

■ This is the second most common form of notarization.

■ The signer must sign the document in the notary's presence.

■ The notary must administer a separate oath for each jurat.

■ Out-of-state jurats aren't acceptable, and a loose-leaf jurat needs to be used.

○ For proof of execution by a subscribing witness certificate, the following specifics are needed:

■ This document is used when the document principal/signer can't personally appear before the notary.

■ This document can't be used on any documents that

affect real property or on documents that require a thumbprint in the notary's journal.

■ The subscribing witness needs to be identified by a credible witness with an acceptable form of identification.

■ There has to be an unbroken chain of personal knowledge:

• The notary needs to know the credible witness, the credible witness needs to know the subscribing witness, and the subscribing witness needs to know the principal.

• Notaries are allowed to notarize documents in any language they can't speak or read since they aren't responsible for the contents of the documents, provided the notarial wording is in English.

• Notaries can't notarize documents for a signer that they are unable to communicate. And they can't use an interpreter.

• When completing a notarization with a signature by mark, the following applies:

○ The process requires two viewing witnesses who

observe the principal/signer making their mark on the document and in the notary's journal.

○ The viewing witnesses don't have to be identified, but they do need the following:

■ They must sign the document as witnesses.

■ The witness must cursive the principal/signer's name next to the mark on the document.

■ The witness or the notary needs to write the principal/signer's name next to the mark in the notary's journal.

• The notary must take, subscribe and file the oath of office and file a surety bond with the county clerk's office or place of business as stated in the application within 30 calendar days from the date of the commission.

• Errors and Omissions Insurance can be purchased to protect a notary who damages someone as a result of notarial misconduct or negligence. This can even be true in the following situations:

○ Even simple oversights like failing to affix a notary

seal or properly identify a principal/signer can subject the notary to being personally liable for losses and/or damages.

• A notary public is allowed to notarize for relatives as long as don't so doesn't provide a direct financial or beneficial interest to the notary.

• The employer of a notary can limit notarization to the following in the ordinary course of employment:

○ Who and when to notarize and

○ How much the notary can charge for their services

• Notaries are prohibited from providing legal advice and/or practice law unless they are also a licensed and practicing attorney.

These are the general facts that apply to notaries in all states. This information forms the basics of what is covered in most notary exams in states that require them. Knowing this information is the first step in helping you pass your notary exams. The next thing you need to do is prepare for your notary exam. Even in states where the exam is a handful of open-book questions, it can be a good idea to prepare and study in advance. Let's consider some practical tips to help you study for and prepare to take the notary exam.

Preparing for the Notary Exam

The notary public is responsible for verifying signatures on important legal and real estate documents. Most states require notaries to have some level of education before getting a commission, and a few states require individuals to take a licensing exam in order to show they understand the basic knowledge of notary laws and the role they play in society. Tests are often done at testing centers in written form or online, and the exact requirements will vary by state. You'll often have plenty of time to prepare for your exam, and the following are some tips to help you prepare for the notary exam if it is required in your state.

Study Guides and Handbooks

The licensing authority of the state in which you want to serve as a notary public will provide guidelines for taking the exam. This will often include a handbook. The handbook for the state will provide all aspects of becoming a notary public, the laws that need to be followed and the specific duties of a notary public as allowed in that state. By studying these handbooks, you can get a good idea of what specific state information may be on the exam in addition to the general guidelines and information we listed above.

Review Notary Public Laws and Recent Cases

You can also research online about notary public laws for your state. This can often be found online at the state legislature home page and a search of the words notary public. This will be the easiest way to find the most recent applicable legislation. The full texts of the laws are often available on the website of the agencies that issue licenses. For example, the Secretary of State in New York provides full texts of their laws online. You can also search for recent court cases that involve potential errors by notaries public so you can have some real-life examples of the application of notary laws.

Study Potential Scenarios

Take a moment to look up frequently asked questions and common requests for notaries. Many state agencies that license notaries will have this information on their websites. For example, California offers these questions and their associated answers online. Playing out potential scenarios is a great way to help you understand the laws and the appropriate actions you should take. This practice can help you when it comes to answering multiple-choice questions related to the decision-making process of notaries. For example, as a notary, you may be asked to notarize a document that you didn't personally view the signing of and choosing the right action in the situation can be a real question on an exam.

Test Questions and Practice Tests

The last thing you can do is consider taking practice

tests and questions. Self-testing can help you check your research and see what areas you need to increase your research. There are paid practice tests you can take online, but for a simple general question test, you can often do this on your own with a few sample questions, such as you'll get in the upcoming practice tests of this book.

All of these things are going to help you prepare for your notary exam. Now let's provide you with some practice tests to get ready for your notary exam. First, we'll provide some general notary exam practice questions and answers for you to prepare with, then we'll look at some specific examples of questions.

General Notary Exam Practice Questions

What is the term for individuals who receive services from notaries?

Constituents.

What services does a notary commonly provide?

Taking acknowledgments, administering oaths and affirmations, executing affidavits and taking depositions.

Are notarized documents admissible in court?

Yes. Documents are considered valid and establish "prima facia" evidence or presumptive evidence.

Is a notary public considered a commissioned public officer?

Yes. The notary public is appointed by the Secretary of State by Executive Law.

Why do people need a notary?

Notaries authenticate signatures, compel truthfulness from others and help to reduce the risk of fraud.

What are notaries NOT responsible for?

A notary isn't responsible for guaranteeing the accuracy or truth of any statements in the documents they are notarizing.

What notarial act is the most commonly performed?

The acknowledgment is found in deeds, mortgages and other associated real estate documents and other areas not related to real estate.

What are the potential sizes for a notary stamp?

Notary stamps should be 1 inch in width and 2 ½ inches in length.

If a regulation states up to 30 days, what does this mean?

This means calendar days.

What shape must a notary stamp be?

A notary stamp must be rectangular in shape.

What are the requirements for two credible witnesses?

There are no specific requirements.

Subscribing witnesses can come to a notary with which documents?

A homestead declaration.

A notary who willingly and knowingly notarizes a fraudulent real estate document is guilty of what?

The notary is guilty of a felony.

A new notary certificate is awarded by whom?

The Secretary of State.

What code allows notaries to certify a copy of a power of attorney?

The Probate Code.

Under the signature-by-mark process, how many people must write the name of the X signer?

At least one individual.

How long do you have to report a move to the proper authority?

You have 30 days.

When making a false statement, what is the statute of limitations?

Four years.

What isn't required on a passport?

The signature of the notary.

An ID must have what?

An ID must have a picture, a physical description and a signature.

Notaries must do what with their journal and stamp?

The journal and stamp must remain under the direct control of the notary.

Where are you to deliver your papers when you resign from a commission?

The county clerk where you have your current oath on file.

What isn't required when taking an oath?

You are not required to raise your right hand.

Notary certificates must be signed by whom?

Certificates must be signed by the notary.

An acceptable ID must be issued within what time frame?

Within the last 5 years.

After giving your journal to the proper authority, you have how long to notify the Secretary of State?

You have 10 days.

When moving, you must contact which authority?

You must contact the Secretary of State.

Who has the authority to take your journal?

A peace officer who has probable cause.

What is a notary not required to do regarding a fee?

A notary is not required to charge a fee.

Which documents require the signer to leave a right thumbprint?

A Power of Attorney and a Trust Deed for real estate.

What is an affirmation?

It is the legal equivalent to an oath but has no referral to a Supreme Being.

What is a notary not allowed to notarize?

A notary cannot notarize real estate documents when they are a mortgagor in a transaction.

A certificate of authorization can be provided by whom?

Only from the Secretary of State.

When it comes to reproductions, what does a certified copy certify?

A certified copy certifies that the reproduction is accurate.

Notaries cannot perform their actions when serving in what other capacity?

Notaries cannot perform services when they are named as a principal in a financial transaction.

What does an acknowledgment certify?

An acknowledgment certifies that a signer's identity was satisfactorily proven, the signer admits to signing the document, and the signer appeared before the notary.

Where do notaries get their seals from?

Only from approved vendors and manufacturers.

Who can bring a document to a notary if the principal is unable to appear?

A subscribing witness.

A subscribing witness is placed under oath and asked what?

The subscribing witness is asked three things: 1) Did you sign as a witness? 2) Did the signer acknowledge their signing? 3) Did the signer ask for the document to be notarized?

When is the term for when a subscribing witness brings the document?

Proof of Execution

If someone inherits property in another state and they need to send an affidavit to the court, what can a notary do?

A notary can do a notarization process.

What must be signed in the presence of a notary?

A Jurat.

If someone influences a notary to perform improperly, they are guilty of what?

They are guilty of a misdemeanor.

An oath is defined as what?

An affirmation or a solemn spoken pledge.

A notary needs to rely on what to provide satisfactory evidence of identity?

ID cards and business card photos.

The notary is obligated to do what?

A notary is required to reimburse a surety company for any bond funds that are paid out.

A notary may perform what additional services?

A notary can notarize documents in a foreign language,

and they can notarize a relative's documents.

Notaries are allowed to withhold services to whom?

A notary working for an employer can limit services to transactions related to the employer's business. A notary may also withhold services if a document is incomplete or if they believe an individual doesn't know what they are signing.

Is an embossed seal required?

An embossed seal is acceptable but not required.

Credible witnesses cannot be linked to a document in which way?

Credible witnesses can't have a financial interest in the document.

When it comes to a military notary, what are the charges?

A military notary can't charge any fees.

What is the employer of a notary allowed to do in regard to the notary journal?

The employer may copy journal entries related to the business in front of the notary.

The security bond for a notary protects whom?

The security bond protects the public.

The Venue in a document refers to which county?

The county where the signer personally appeared.

What should a notary do if they are asked to notarize an incomplete document?

A notary should refuse to notarize the document.

What is the most commonly completed form?

An acknowledgment.

What items must be recorded in a journal each time?

The date, time, type of document and fees.

A notary cannot advertise what?

A notary cannot advertise the Spanish terms *notario publico* or *notario.*

A credible identifying witness serves what main

purpose?

The credible identifying witness serves to identify the signer.

The seal must include what elements?

The seal must include three elements: 1) The state seal and the notary's name. 2) The expiration date of the commission and county where the oath is on file. 3) A sequential ID number of the manufacturer and the notary's sequential commission number.

An individual who is starting a business as an immigration consultant cannot advertise what?

They cannot advertise themselves as a notary public.

The notary seal must contain what?

The notary seal must contain three elements: 1) Be

photographically reproducible and have an expiration date. 2) Contain the state seal and the words notary public. 3) Have a serrated or milled edge border.

What must a notary do if the signer can't provide a right thumbprint?

The notary may use the left thumb or any available finger as long as a note of the problem is provided.

Which documents don't require a seal?

A seal isn't required on subdivision maps.

After a request for a transaction, the notary has how many days to respond?

Fifteen days.

Someone who poses as a notary but is not commissioned is guilty of what?

A misdemeanor.

A notary who resigns their position with an employer must do what?

The notary must notify the Secretary of State of any business address change.

Why must there be two witnesses for a signature by mark?

To view or acknowledge the making of the mark.

What must be included in a written request for a photocopy of a journal entry?

The type of document, month and year of notarization and names of the parties involved.

If a notary and private employer enter into an agreement, then what happens in regard to notary actions?

Notary actions are limited to business transactions.

What documents can't a notary certify?

A journal entry requested by a member of the public.

Proof of execution can be done on which document?

A Deed of Reconveyance.

The name on the Subscribed and Sworn line of a certificate is whose?

The name of the signer.

A notary and their employer have what right?

To limit notary services solely to their business.

A notary cannot charge a fee for which notarizations?

A circulator's affidavit.

Notaries who engage in an unauthorized practice can have their commission?

Denied, revoked or suspended.

What may the notary use their commission for?

The notary may use their commission to notarize for veterans.

If a notary uses the term notario publico in an advertisement, then their commission can be what?

Suspended for no less than one year and revoked after two offenses.

Under what circumstances can a notary not be automatically disqualified from performing a notarization?

When the notary is serving as a real estate agent.

A notary who doesn't deliver their papers to the county clerk after their commission expires is guilty of what?

A misdemeanor.

A driver's license that has been expired for 52 months is presented to a notary; what should the notary do?

The notary can use it as an acceptable form of

identification.

The right thumbprint isn't needed in the journal for which situation?

In a Deed of Reconveyance.

When notarizing documents for friends, a notary needs to make what note in their journal?

The signer's driver's license number, the type of document and the notary's fee.

Under what circumstances can a commission be suspended and/or revoked?

When a notary doesn't pay child support.

A notary can notarize for a family member when they

are acting in what role?

When the notary is acting as an employee.

When making a witness swear an oath, what phrase can be used?

The phrase "under penalty of perjury."

Should a notary public die, their personal representative must do what?

They should promptly notify the Secretary of State and send all papers and records to the county where the notary's oath is recorded.

When a signer is making a signature by mark, what must happen?

The signer must place their mark in the notary's journal.

What must be included in a journal?

The character of each document.

If the last day for filing an instrument or other document falls on a Saturday or holiday, the act should be performed; when?

By the next business day.

If the notary's certificate is previously filled with an incorrect state and county, what must the notary do?

A line must be drawn through the inappropriate words with the correct state and county then being written in the document.

What is the main purpose of an acknowledgment?

To authenticate signatures and require a personal appearance.

If a person coerces a notary to perform improperly, they are guilty of what?

A misdemeanor.

What doesn't a notary need to record in their journals?

The signer's address.

If the credible witness knows both the signer and the notary personally, then what happens?

Only one witness will be needed.

A notary public can notarize a document if they have done what?

If a document is in a foreign language.

A notary cannot charge fees when verifying what document?

A nomination document or circulator's affidavit.

What is a notary allowed to do if their employer asks to see the journal used in the business to see who is providing the most business?

The employer is allowed to only see items that pertain to the business.

A notary can notarize documents that will be filed in another state, but they can't do what?

They can't certify the signer holds a particular capacity.

If a notary works for a city, county or state agency, then fees collected for non-agency notarizations go to whom?

The notary public must remit them to the employing agency.

What must the notary do when notarizing a document containing an acknowledgment?

The notary may accept a document that has already been signed.

When should an oath be involved in an acknowledgment?

When the signer uses a credible witness as their form of ID.

The notary should accept what to establish the proper

ID of the principal?

The notary can accept one of three things: 1) Two credible witnesses with IDs who personally know the principal. 2) A credible witness who personally knows the notary and the principal with proper ID. 3) A proper ID from the principal that is current or issued within the last five years.

What additional item is needed with a foreign passport?

A stamp from a US Immigration Agency.

If a notary faces a judgment of $22,000 and their bond pays $15,000, then how much is the notary liable for?

The notary is liable for $22,000.

How is a subscribing witness identified?

By one credible witness known to the subscribing witness and the notary with an ID.

A notary seal and signature can't be affixed to a document without what?

Notarial wording.

Foreign language advertising regulations have strict rules with one exception?

A single desk plaque.

The Secretary of State will give written notice when a check isn't honored for payment. With no correction, the second notice of cancellation is effective when?

In 20 days.

If a public agency pays the employee's expenses, then what happens with the fees?

The fees are remitted to the agency.

What must a notary do if they are unable to communicate with a customer?

The notary should refer them to someone who speaks their language.

What key wording is found in an acknowledgment?

Personally appeared.

A notary needs to do what in order to meet the 30 calendar day filing limit for the oath with the county?

The notary should allow for any type of delay.

What are the exceptions to an appearance by the principal?

A subscribing witness.

What is one main purpose of a jurat?

It is to make sure the signer signs in front of the notary.

How must the notary communicate a change in address to the Secretary of State?

This can be done in one of three ways: 1) The notary must communicate the change when it is a business address. 2) The notary must communicate the change when it is a residential address. 3) The communication must be by certified mail within 30 days.

What is an attest or attestation?

The completion of a certificate by a notary who has done a notarial act.

What is a commission?

It is the empowerment to perform notarial acts and the written evidence of authority to perform said acts.

What is an acknowledgment?

It is a notarial act in which the notary certifies that three things occurred: 1) The individual appeared before the notary. 2) The individual is personally known by the notary or identified through satisfactory evidence. 3) The signature was the individual, and the signed record was done in the presence of the notary.

What is a commissioning date?

It is the date entered on the commissioning or

recommissioning certificate for a notary.

What is an appointment or appoint?

It is the process of naming an individual to the office of notary public after determining the individual has complied with all requirements.

What are the various definitions and levels of a crime?

A crime can be defined in five different levels: 1) An attempt to commit a crime. 2) An accessory to the commission of a crime. 3) Aiding and abetting a crime. 4) Conspiracy to commit a crime. 5) Solicitation to commit a crime.

What is a jurat?

A notary certificate that evidences the administration of an oath or affirmation.

What is an appointee?

It is an individual who has been appointed or reappointed to the office of notary public but hasn't yet taken the oath of office to be commissioned.

What does an acknowledgment acknowledge?

The acknowledgment provides three things: 1) The individual appeared in person and provided a record. 2) The individual was personally known to the notary. 3) The document was signed while in the physical presence of the notary or indicates that the signature is their own.

Who is an applicant?

A person who seeks an appointment or reappointment to the office of notary public.

Who is a credible witness?

An individual who is personally known to the notary and to whom two things apply: 1) The notary believes the individual is honest and reliable. 2) The notary believes the person is not a party to or a beneficiary of the transaction.

What is an affirmation?

A notarial act that is the legal equivalent to an oath in which the notary certifies that at a single time and place, the following occurred: 1) The individual appeared in person. 2) The individual was either known to the notary or provided the required identification. 3) The individual made a vow of truthfulness under penalty of perjury based on personal honor and without invoking a deity or using any form of the word "swear."

What is an attestation?

It is the completion of a certificate by a notary after

performing a notarial act.

How long must a notary retain their journal?

Ten years.

If a notary receives a document that doesn't have a notary certificate, they should do what?

The notary should ask the signer to determine the type of certificate based on the plain meaning of notarial acts.

If someone requests to view the notary journal, they may only do so under what circumstances?

It must be within the physical presence of the notary.

If a document isn't in English but has a notarial certificate in English, can a notary still notarize the document?

Yes.

When a notary's commission is revoked by the
Secretary of State, what happens?

Three things happen: 1) You are not allowed to receive
a notary commission in any state. 2) You must follow the
legal resignation rules. 3) You can be at risk for civil and
criminal liability.

If a notary is not a lawyer, they can't do what?

A notary who isn't a lawyer can't do three things: 1)
Advise a client which certificate to use on a document. 2)
Engage in any unauthorized practice of law. 3) Advertise
yourself as an expert in immigration matters.

New York State Notary Exam

The toughest state exam for a notary is New York. Applicants are required to pass the exam with a minimum score of 70 percent in order to be awarded their commission. There is no required training in New York, so individuals need to learn the material covered in the exam on their own. The exam is timed and closely monitored so you'll need to be prepared to complete it within an hour. During the exam, no notes, books or reference aids are allowed and you need to turn off all electronic devices. Below you'll find two practice tests to help you test your knowledge with potential questions from the New York state notary exam.

How long is a notary public commission?

A commission is a four year term.

How is a notary public commissioned renewed?

Renewal can be completed without re-taking the exam as long as paperwork is submitted within six months of the expiration of the term.

What is the jurisdiction for a notary in the state of New York?

All 62 counties of the state.

What happens if a constituent outside of New York is

seeking the help of a state commissioned notary?

The meeting between the constituent and notary must take place within the boundaries of the state. A New York state notary cannot travel to other states to perform any notary duty unless they are commissioned or licensed in those states as well.

Who is prohibited from becoming a notary in the state of New York?

State law prohibits sheriffs from any county from holding other public offices. Convicted felons may not become a public notary.

A practicing attorney in New York needs to take what exam to become a notary?

Attorneys who are admitted to the New York State Bar and who are actively practicing in the state don't need to take the state notary exam, but they must submit an application and pay any associated fees.

Do court clerks get commissioned as notaries?

No. However, court clerks who have taken the Civil Service promotional exam don't have to take the state notary exam. They do still need to submit an application and pay any associated fees.

Notary Exam Test Taking Tips

When it comes to taking any exam, there are certain things you can do to increase your chances of passing the test. So consider the following tips when taking your notary exam, so you are able to pass your exam.

• When taking the test, it is important to stay relaxed and have a positive attitude.

• Maintain focus on your own test and not the test of others around you.

• Take the time to determine the concept that the question is testing.

• After reading the question, come up with a likely answer in your head and then read the potential answers. This helps to avoid getting sidetracked or confused by the choices provided on the test.

• Look for any overriding rules; this can be helpful when faced with word problems and scenarios.

• If you are faced with a scenario, you should take a moment to determine who the notary is in the scenario.

• Always choose the best answer. Use a process of elimination from the choices given and then choose the best answer.

• If you aren't completely sure of the answer to a question, then skip it for the moment. Sometimes other questions in the test will help you answer a question. Just make sure you come back to answer the question. An unanswered question is always going to be wrong, but taking a random guess will give you at least a 25% chance of getting a correct answer.

- Always choose the answer that is most whole and complete, which means it can stand on its own.

- Always check for keywords in the question, such as except, all, not, all except and other similar keywords. Read the test question once to look for these keywords and note and/or circle them. Then re-read the question. Then look at all potential answers before making your final choice.

- Look for all of the above and/or none of the above answer choices. If you are certain one statement is true, then don't choose none of the above as an answer, or if you know a statement is false, then don't select all of the above as an answer.

- Avoid reading into the question. Answer only what the question asks of you. Something may be correct or incorrect, but is that what the question is asking?

- If the question names a specific document, then determine any special conditions and/or limitations that pertain to that document, such as those listed in our study guide earlier.

- Often, the correct answer is going to be the choice

with the most information.

• A positive choice is often going to be more true than a negative choice.

• Always ask yourself if the answer makes sense and covers the whole problem.

• When all else fails, go with your gut instinct when choosing an answer.

So now you hopefully know what a notary job entails and have seen why going this route is a good idea for you. Then hopefully, we have shown you what you are likely to need to know for a notary exam. Finally, take the time to go through the practice tests as often as possible until you are ready to take the test. Then use the tips at the end of this book to help you pass your notary exam on the first try and start your new job.

Part 2: New York Notary Public Exam Study Guide

This is a guidebook to assist you with the Notary Public Exam in New York State. The formal booklet is available online but contains a huge amount of legal jargon and confusing terminology. Here we have simplified the text and highlighted what you MUST know for the exam. In addition, we have provided the most common questions that are most likely to be asked in the test. NYS places a heavy emphasis on definitions, and it is important to know the meaning of all the legal terms in the text below.

Appointment and Qualifications

The Process of Becoming a Notary in New York State

The term of office is four years.

Unlike several other states, esp California, there is no need for the notary public to obtain a notary bond, notary seal, or a notary journal.

There is no study course required before taking the

exam.

All notary public appointments are regulated by the Secretary of State

Eligibility Criteria

Be at least age 18

Have a good moral character.

Have a business office or Reside in New York State

Have, at a minimum common school education.

Not have any convictions- however, it depends on the type of crime, and the Secretary of State makes the ultimate decision.

After passing the exam, one has to be appointed as Notary Public. However, at this time, applicants need to be either American citizens or permanent residents. Illegal immigrants cannot become a notary public in NYS.

The Exam

Closed book proctored exam

One hour

Photo ID needed for the exam

All test takers have to submit thumbprints

The exam fee is $15

Need 70% to pass

After passing the exam, one needs to download the application form

$60 application fee and will include the oath of office, which has to be sworn to and notarized.

Note for the initial application, the fee is sent to the Secretary of State. For subsequent reappointments, the fee is submitted to the County Clerk.

If the application is approved, a new commission is mailed

It will be sent over to the applicant within 4-6 weeks

New York Notary Law

To be eligible for work in other counties, The NY notary public may file a certificate of official character and sample signature with the county clerk of any county for a fee of $10

A certificate of official character is then issued by the Secretary of State for a fee of $10 or the county where the notary first qualified for a fee of $5.

Non Residents

Individuals who reside in other states but have a place of business in New York state can work as a notary public in NYS.

The oath of office and signature of these notaries must be filed in the county where he or she intends to practice.

Reappointment

A renewal form is set to the notary about three months

prior to the expiration of the commission.

Renewals cost $60

Change of Status

If the notary public decides to exit New York State but still retains a bona fide business office in the State, he or she can still work as a notary public. However, if the business closes, the commission will be vacated.

If a non-resident notary public ceases to have an office in New York, the office of the notary is vacated.

Name and address change in State: if a notary public moves within the State, there is a $10 fee for the address change notice

The fee is not required if the individual name change is due to a change in marital status.

It is also not mandatory to notify the Division of licensing services immediately of a name or address change. The name can be changed during the reappointment of a new commission.

The name change does require proof such as a marriage certificate, driver's license, passport, etc.

Marriage and Name Change

If the notary public gets married during the term of office, he or she may continue to use the same name to which he or she was commissioned. But if she elects to use the married name, then for the duration of the term, the notary must continue to use the same name which he or she was commissioned in the signature and seal but can add his or her signature to the married name in parentheses. When renewing the commission, he or she can then apply under the married name or name under which he or she was first commissioned.

Change of Email Address

Within five days after the change of an electronic notary's email, the notary must notify the Secretary of State of the address change.

No notary can perform all notarial transactions exclusively with electronic notarization.

A notary may refuse electronic notarization if 1) he is not satisfied that the principal is competent or 2) the principal signature is voluntarily made.

Appointment Highlights

A notary public in NYS can only be appointed by the Secretary of State

The term of the commission is for four years.

At the time of application, the individual must have a place to conduct business or an office in New York State. Or the individual must be a resident of the State.

Even if a notary moves out of State but maintains an office in NYS, he or she can still practice in the State as a notary public. However, if the notary public moves out of State and does not retain his or her office, he will need to vacate the office as a notary public.

Once a notary public has the commission removed by the Secretary of State, that individual will not be eligible for another appointment. The removal is usually permanent.

All notary publics who have been removed from office or have the commission dismissed shall remove all signs of the commission -or it can lead to a misdemeanor charge.

The Appointment Process

All applicants need to submit the application to the Secretary of State.

Individuals of good character are appointed as notaries. These individuals will need to have their official signature and oath of office filed.

There is a non-refundable fee of $60

A successful application will result in a notary public ID card.

A certified copy of the original oath and official signature and $20 taken from the initial fee will be transmitted by the Secretary of State to the county where the appointee will reside.

For reappointments, the Secretary will submit to the county clerk the application for the oath of office with the signature.

If the application or reappointment is satisfactory, the clerk will issue the commission.

The date of commission, a certified copy of the application, and $40 from the original fee will be transmitted by the county clerk to the Secretary of State, who will make a proper record of the commission.

The Secretary of State will receive a non-refundable fee of $10 for changing the same address of the notary public.

Reappointments

If the notary seeks a reappointment, he has up to 6 months after the commission has expired order to have the qualifying requirements waived by the Secretary of State.

Further, if the application of reappointment is filed after the expiration period and the individual is inducted or enlisted in the armed forces, such qualifying requirements may be waived by the Secretary of State. However, the application for reappointment has to be made within a period of 1 year after discharge; at the same time, the discharge from the military must be satisfactory and NOT dishonorable.

Executive Law

The seal and signature of a county clerk on the certificate of an official character of a notary public may be printed, facsimile, stamped, printed, engraved, or photographed.

In NYS, a notary public is appointed by the Secretary of State.

Duties of a Notary Public

Can work within the jurisdiction of NYS, but the practice is limited to the county where registered

Administer affirmations and oaths

Take affidavits and depositions

Receive and certify acknowledgments, proof of deeds, power of attorney, mortgages

Demand payment and protest the non-acceptance or non-payment

A notary public who is a lawyer can practice law in the State

For any misconduct, the notary public is liable to parties that have been injured

Fraud

Without an appointment by the Secretary of State, one cannot act as a notary public.

One cannot advertise that he or she is a notary public when formally, there is no appointment.

Practicing as a notary public without a commission is fraud, and one can be charged with a misdemeanor.

Acting or pretending to be a holder of a commissioner of deeds or notary public is a crime.

Notary Public Disqualifications

Disqualification of a notary public is not rare.

A notary public should not have a financial interest in the instrument they affirm or certify. If there appears to be a conflict of interest, the notary public should rescue himself.

A notary public who is a beneficiary interested in the conveyance by way of being secured should not take an acknowledgment of the instrument.

If there is misconduct by the notary public, he or she can be liable to the injured parties for the damages.

Protest

The notary may protest a non-bill payment with a notice; the fee for the initial protest is $0.75, and 10 cents for each notice. No more than five notices can be submitted.

The notary public may affix a seal to the protest at no cost.

All notaries who have a seal shall affix the seal to such protest at no cost.

Removal

If there is misconduct by the notary public, such as fraud or deceit, he or she can be guilty of a misdemeanor and may be removed from office.

The Secretary of State has the power to remove or suspend a notary public for misconduct.

In all cases, prior to the removal of the notary public, the individual will be served with a copy of the charges and have the opportunity to present his or her side of the story.

Any person with a prior conviction is not eligible to become a notary public in NYS. Because there are many types of crimes, only the Secretary of State can determine who can become a notary public following a conviction. For example, if you committed forgery, then there is no chance, but if you injured a pedestrian while riding your bike, then the Secretary of State will decide on the seriousness of the case. A person with a felony can never be a notary public in NYS.

A lawyer can function as a notary public but must have his office within the State.

Certificate of the Official Character of the Notary Public

The county clerk or Secretary of State may certify the official character of the notary public.

For each office certificate of character, the Secretary of State will collect one dollar.

Certification of Notarial Signatures

Upon payment of a $3 fee, the county clerk can provide an official certificate of the notary's signature.

Electronic Notarization

Electronic notarization is permitted in NYS.

If a notary public wants to perform electronic notarial acts, he or she must do the following:

All notary publics who want to notarize electronically must first register with the State and prove that they have the capability and technology to safely and securely notarize electronically. NYS has several compliance factors for electronic technology use that must be satisfied.

The notary public can use only providers and vendors who comply with the standards set by the State

The notary public must be physically located within New York State

Use a network that allows location detection when performing a notarial act

Affix a reliable electronic signature to electronic records

The Electronic Signature and Identification

It must be unique to the notary public

Be attached to the electronic certificate.

Be under the control of the notary public.

Be linked to data that detect any alterations of the signature.

The notary public must use the electron signature only for notarial acts.

Ensure that the person making the acknowledgment is the one who appeared using communication technology.

If the principal is located outside the State, the individual's Identity must be verified through verbal communication.

Any notice of change must be electronically transmitted to the Secretary of State and signed with the notary's electronic signature.

Satisfactory Evidence of Identity

The notary public may obtain satisfactory evidence of the identity of the individual who signs a document. This may include the following:

Have the signer show a photo ID. Both the front and back of the ID card must be examined.

The card must be current and valid.

The ID must have a photographic image of the signer.

The ID must reveal an accurate description of the signer.

The ID card should have the signature of the signer.

The notary must look at two current documents that may have the signer's signature.

The notary may want to attest that the individual is known to him.

Take the oath or affirmation of a witness who knows the individual and notary public.

Takes the oath or affirmation of two witnesses who personally know the individual and provide ID.

If the individual signing the documents appears before an electronic notary, satisfactory evidence includes the following:

Verify the ID utilizing communication technology.

Undertake credential analysis.

Use a third-party provider to identify the individual.

Credential Analysis

Must be performed by a third-party service provider who can provide evidence to the online notary public of the provider's ability to satisfy the requirements.

Credential analysis usually utilizes private and public data to confirm the validity of the ID credentials and must use the following:

Automated software to aid the notary public in verifying the ID of the remote individual.

Ensure that the ID credential passes an authenticity test.

Utilizes technology that includes visual, physical, and cryptographic features.

Use technology to confirm that the ID credential is not modified or fraudulent.

Uses information from an authoritative source.

Provides an output of the authenticity test to the online notary.

Communication Technology

It must have adequate visual and audio clarity so that the notary public and the individual can see and speak to each other.

At the same time, this should allow for ID verification, proofing, and application of notary signature and seal without interruption.

The system should have adequate visual clarity so that the notary can read, view and capture the back and front text of the ID card.

The signal transmission should be secure.

Should allow for reproduction but not permit deletions, additions, or changes in the record

Allows recording and archiving of the audio-video communication session

Allows the notary to keep a copy of the recording

The recording should not display or discuss any personal ID information.

The recording must be kept for at least ten years from the date of the transaction.

Recordkeeping and Reporting- Electronic and Paper Records

All notaries must maintain records to document compliance.

Record storage can be done with a third party as long as it is secure

All stored records should include the following:

Date, time, and type of notarial act

Name and address of the individual for whom the notarial act was done

Type and number of notarial services provided

Type of credentials used to identify the principal

The verification procedure used for all personal appearances

For electronic records, the ID of communication technology, certification authority, and verification providers utilized

All electronic records (both audio and video) must be safely stored and retained for at least ten years

Records must be reproduced for the Secretary of State in case there is an audit or query

Applications for Electronic Notarization and Renewals

Before a notary public can provide electronic services, he must be appointed and commissioned by the Secretary of State.

The term of service is for four years.

No notary public can perform electronic notarial acts without first registering and demonstrating the capability to notarize electronically.

To be approved for electronic notarial acts, the following is necessary:

Supply name and address to Secretary of State.

In addition, the principal must have a signature that is reflected on record, that it is notarized, and that he has taken an oath administered by the notary.

Send the expiration date of the commission and signature to the Secretary.

Submit the notary's email address.

Description of the electronic technology that is going to be used and the sample of the electronic signature.

The notary can apply for reappointment within 90 days of the expiration of the commission.

All information sent to the Secretary of State has to be accurate - failure to comply can mean no reappointment.

The same paper-based methods to identify document signers apply to electronic notarization. However, when using communication technology, the standards have to be approved by the Secretary of state and meet the following criteria:

Signal transmission is secure and free from interception.

Signal technology allows the notary to communicate with the principal in real time.

The communication technology will allow the notary to communicate with and identify the remotely located individual.

The system allows for two or more different processes for authenticating the identity of the remotely located individual.

The notary must keep the video and audio records on file for at least ten years.

Prior to performing any electronic notarial act, the notary public has to formally register with the Secretary of State and complete an application that has a fee.

Types of electronic notarial acts allowed:

Execution of any instrument in writing

The notary public must be located within the state of

New York, regardless of where the signer is located.

If the principal is located outside the US, the record of the notarial act filed by the notary shall involve property located in the US or connected to the US.

Fees

All applicants must submit a $60 non-refundable fee when applying for a notary position

Registrants for electronic notarial acts must submit a non-refundable $60 registration fee

For renewals, there is a non-refundable $60 fee

All notary publics must take the written exam and have to submit a $15 fee for each test

The fee for change requests and duplicate license registration is $10

The notary public is allowed to charge a fee for his services

An electronic notary public can charge a fee of $25 for

each electronic notarial act

Sentence for Felony

The maximum sentence is imprisonment for a term of at least three years

For class D felony, the term will not exceed seven years

For class E felony, the term shall not exceed four years

Sentence of Misdemeanor Violations

Class A misdemeanor sentence will not exceed more than one year

Forgery in the 2nd Degree

A person is guilty of second-degree forgery when with intent to defraud, he also falsely makes and alters a written instrument. This may include a deed, codicil, will, contract, commercial instrument, or assignee, which may create, transfer, or terminate an otherwise legal right, interest, or obligation.

Forgery is a class D felony.

Issuing a False Certificate

Notaries are committing a crime when issuing a false certificate. This is a class E felony.

Official Misconduct

A notary is guilty of official misconduct when he or she commits unauthorized exercise of his official functions.

Knowingly refrains from conducting duty imposed upon him by law. A notary public must officiate on request.

Once a notary is commissioned and takes an oath, he or she is bound by law to administer the service when requested- refusal to do so is a misdemeanor.

Perjury

A notary can be guilty of perjury if he takes an oath and then gives false testimony.

Election Law

A commissioner of elections or inspector of elections is eligible for the office of a notary public.

An oath is a verbal pledge that an individual takes when providing a statement.

Under oath, the individual is supposed to provide an honest statement or risk punishment if the statements are false.

Notaries usually administer oaths and affirmations but take into consideration the individual's ethical or religious beliefs.

An oath requires the person physically appear before a notary. It cannot be administered over the phone. Plus, the oath has to be administered in a formal manner as required by law.

The person taking the oath must express the words 'I do.'

For the oath to be valid:

The individual swearing or affirming must physically be present in the presence of a notary public.

The individual swears that what he states is true.

The individual conscientiously takes upon himself the obligation of an oath.

The notary public does not fulfill his duty if he simply asks the individual if the signature on the affidavit is his- an oath has to be formally administered.

A partnership or corporation cannot take an oath–it has to be an individual.

A notary cannot administer an oath to himself.

The privileges and rights of a notary public are personal and cannot be delegated to any other person.

Public Officers Law

Notarial Acts

Notaries in New York State can perform the following notarial services:

Take proofs and acknowledgments

Administer affirmations and oaths

Take depositions and affidavits

Demand acceptance of payment

Protest for non-payment

Be present when a safe deposit box is opened and take an inventory of the contents. Must create a document with the list of contents, etc

Acknowledgments

It is defined as an act where the individual named in the instrument tells the notary that he or she is the individual named in the instrument and acknowledges that he executed the instrument.

As part of the process, the notary public also obtains satisfactory evidence of the identity of the individual whose acknowledgment is taken.

The notary public will certify that he or she has taken the acknowledgment by signing the form.

The subscribing witness will state his or her place of residence, that he knows the individual described, who executed the instrument, and he visually saw the individual execute the instrument.

If a notary is going to be executing functions of public

office, he or she must take the oath. Failure to do so can lead to a misdemeanor charge.

Fees of Public Officers

Notaries can only be compensated by fees that are allowed by law.

If there is no fee established, the notary must execute the same without a reward or fee.

Notaries are not allowed to charge more fees than those stated by law.

Notaries cannot demand fees for referrals unless he or she has provided the service.

Violations of the fee law provisions may result in treble damages to the plaintiff.

Notaries subject themselves to criminal prosecution, possible removal, or a civil suit by asking for higher fees than the stated allowance.

Notaries are not entitled to a fee for administering an oath to a member of the legislature, to any inspector of election, military officer, poll clerk, or to any public officer or public employee.

Fees for Public Officers

The notary public can only charge what the state has recommended for notarial services.

If there is no fee set by the Secretary of State, then the Notary public should not charge a fee.

A fee for notarial services should only be demanded if the act was performed.

Charging higher fees can result in a crime, and the notary may be liable for treble damages to the plaintiff.

Penalties may include loss of commission, criminal prosecution, and a civil suit.

Public officers should not charge a fee for administering an oath to a military officer, member of the legislature, clerk of the poll, inspector of election, or any other public employee.

County Law

The county clerk can designate staff members to act as a notary public to notarize documents for the public in the county clerk's office during business hours for free.

The individual appointed as a notary public is exempt from the examination and application fee.

Only one person is selected to work as a notary public.

Anyone with a prior conviction is not eligible for the office of a notary public.

A notary public may be an office, public servant, director, stockholder or employee of a business, deputy clerk, mayor, recorder of the city, etc., and can take proof or an acknowledgment or administer an oath.

However, if any of the above people have any interest in the corporation or financial interest, he or she is not allowed to take an acknowledgment or proof.

The Invalidity of Notary Acts

In most cases, minor errors, typos, or spelling mistakes do not invalidate an instrument that has been notarized.

If the person has not been commissioned as a notary public, the instrument notarized is invalid.

Major mistakes in the name of the person can also invalidate the instrument.

Failing to take the oath is also a reason for an invalid instrument.

If the notary public's term has expired, then the notarization acts may also be invalid.

Vacating the office and moving in or out of state, or changing the address can also lead to the invalidity of the instrument.

Working outside the jurisdiction of the appointment can also lead to an invalid instrument.

When it comes time for renewal of the commission, the individual has up to 6 months after the date of expiration to reapply. If done within six months, there is no need to restart the whole process again. The reapplication for a notary public goes to the County Clerk where first registered and NOT to the Secretary of State.

Official Misconduct

A notary public can be guilty of official misconduct if he benefits or harms another individual

Commits unauthorized acts of official functions

Knowingly refuses to perform notarial acts

A notary public can be guilty of 2nd-degree forgery if he intentionally deceives, defrauds, or injures another party by altering or changing a written instrument (e.g., deed, will, contract, codicil, etc.)

2nd-degree forgery is a class D Felony

Issuing a false certificate with an intent to deceive, defraud or injure another person is a crime and is considered a class E felony.

Judiciary Law

Other than lawyers, no one else can practice law. Preparing deeds, mortgages, discharges, leases, assignments, or any other instrument that affects wills, real estate, codicils, or instruments that affect the disposition of property is performed by lawyers and not notaries.

Individuals who violate these provisions can be guilty of a misdemeanor.

Practicing law in NYS without being a lawyer is a crime.

Notaries cannot execute Wills either, as it is considered an invasion of the practice of law.

Banking Law

All safe deposit boxes in a bank have a rental fee, and if the fee is not paid or the lease is terminated, the box has to be emptied.

The owner of the safe deposit box (lessee) has to be given at least 30 days' notice after lease termination before the deposit box can be opened.

A notary public has to be present during the opening of the safe deposit box.

The notary public will take an inventory, write the

name of the bank and itemize what has been found.

Within ten days, a copy of this certificate has to be mailed to the lessee at the last known address.

Domestic Relations Law

A notary public does not have the authority to solemnize marriages in NYS; In addition, he or she cannot take the acknowledgment of parties and witnesses to a written contract of marriage.

Sheriffs cannot hold another public office in NYS.

Illegal practice of law by a notary public.

A notary public cannot practice as a lawyer if he has not been trained to do- it is a crime

A notary public cannot even offer legal advice on legal matters if not trained as a lawyer

A notary public cannot draft a will

A notary public cannot advertise that he or she is a lawyer when not trained to do so

Civil Practice Law and Rules

A notary public can take a deposition in a civil proceeding.

A notary cannot perform a marriage ceremony. Nor can a notary public take the acknowledgment of the witnesses and parties to a written contract of marriage

Notaries are entitled to fees for the following:

Administering an oath or affirmation

Obtaining and certifying the acknowledgment or proof of execution of a written instrument by one individual ($2) and for each additional individual $2, for swearing such witness $2

For electronic notarial services, the fee set by the Secretary of State

Schedule of Fees

Appointment as Notary Public–

Total Commission Fee $60.00

($40 appointment and $20 filing of Oath of Office)

Change of Name/Address $10.00

Duplicate Identification Card $10.00

Issuance of Certificate of Official Character $1.00

Filing Certificate of Official Character $1.00

Authentication Certificate $3.00

Protest of Note, Commercial Paper, etc. $0.75

Each additional Notice of Protest (limit 5) each $0.10

Oath or Affirmation $2.00

Acknowledgment (each person) $2.00

Proof of Execution (each person) $2.00

Swearing Witness $2.00

Advertising by Notary Public

If a notary does advertise in a language other than English, he must add a disclaimer that he is not a lawyer and is not able to give legal advice on immigration or any legal matters. Further, he cannot accept any money for legal advice.

If a notary advertises in a foreign language, he must add a disclaimer that he is not a lawyer and is not able to give legal advice or accept fees.

A notary cannot use foreign terms when advertising that implies that he or she may be a lawyer.

Advertisement usually means brochures, business cards, notices, etc., whether in electronic or print forms.

False advertising or misrepresentation, as always, is associated with a civil penalty of $1,000

A second violation may result in the suspension of the notary commission, and a third violation may be associated with ever more severe penalties.

Professional Conduct: Rules & Regulations

Satisfy requirements as per Executive law.

Must always get satisfactory evidence to determine the identity of the principal or any individual appearing before the notary.

Require the personal appearance of all individuals for any transaction involving a notarial act.

Administer an oath or affirmation and affix to each instrument the notary's public official number.

Forego the notary act if the individual has an indirect or direct pecuniary interest in the transaction.

Should have no hesitation in refusing to provide notarial services if the requirements are not met or if the notary is not satisfied that the principal has not presented appropriate ID documents.

Maintain notary records as required.

Within five days after a name, address, or email change, submit a written letter to the Secretary of State notifying the change in name or address. The letter must be signed with the notary's official public signature.

A notary can refuse to perform a notarial act if:

The principal is not competent, or the mental capacity to execute a record is in doubt.

The principal's signature may not be voluntarily made.

Use of the office of a notary is limited to notarial acts. It is a serious offense to use the commission for non-notarial activities.

Taking affidavits and acknowledgments over the phone or related devices without the actual physical presence of the individual making the acknowledgment is illegal.

Also unacceptable is the slipshod administration of oaths. Whatever form of administration of the oath, it has to be in the presence of a notary, and it must be an unequivocal and present act

Unless the individual is trained as a lawyer, he or she

cannot engage indirectly or directly in the practice of law.

A notary cannot give advice on legal matters.

The notary is not permitted to draw any kind of legal documents, including deeds, wills, mortgages, bills of sale, chattel mortgages, leases, contracts, liens, releases, power of attorneys, papers in summary proceedings to evict a tenant, or in bankruptcy.

The notary cannot ask for legal referrals from a lawyer he or she may know.

The notary is not permitted to divide or agree on fee splits with a lawyer for referrals.

The notary is not allowed to advertise in any manner or inform others that he has legal powers or rights.

A notary is not allowed to execute an acknowledgment of the execution of a will; this is not the same as the equivalent of an attestation clause accompanying a will.

Statement as to the authority of the notary public:

When completing a notarial act, the notary must type,

print or affix his or her signature in BLACK ink and then write the words 'Notary Public State of New York, name of the county, expiration date of the commission. And where he or she was certified from –the county

In addition, the notary must also affix the official number in black ink.

If the notary wilfully fails to comply with these provisions, he or she can face disciplinary actions.

Notaries can take acknowledgment or proof of stockholder, etc., and can even protest for non-payment bills etc. But a notary cannot take an acknowledgment or proof of a party either individually or as a representative of a company if he or she has a financial interest in the company.

In addition, notaries should not take acknowledgments or proof of deeds of mortgages relating to real estate property.

Validity of Notarial acts:

To perform notarial acts, the individual has to be a notary public or commissioner of deeds.

Misspellings or misnomers of names or other errors can lead to the invalidity of the document

If the notary fails to take or file his official oath, this can result in the invalidity of his commission.

Practicing after the term has expired

Vacating office and going to another public office or. practicing outside the jurisdiction where the notary was authorized to act

Real Property Law

The term "conveyance" is inclusive of all written instruments through which any interest or estate in real property is transferred, created, assigned or mortgaged or through which the real estate property title may be affected during the execution of power or subordinating a mortgage lien. The term is widely used in transactions that involve real estate when sellers and buyers transfer the ownership of a home, building or land.

Acknowledgment and proof of conveyance of real property located in NYS can be done:

At any place within NYS and before a

An official examiner of the title

A notary public

Official referee

Justice of the supreme court

Acknowledgments and proofs of conveyance of real property can be done by both unmarried and married women.

If the public officer is guilty of malfeasance, he or she can be liable for damage to the injured party.

An acknowledgment can only be taken if the notary has satisfactory evidence that the individual making it is the individual described in the instrument.

When there is the execution of a conveyance by a subscribing witness, he or she must state his or her residential address and that he knows the individual described in and who executed the conveyance.

Proof should only be taken if the notary knows the witness or has satisfactory evidence.

Certificate of acknowledgment: The individual taking the acknowledgment or proof of conveyance must attach a signed certificate stating all the proof and testimony of each witness and their residence.

Legal Term Glossary

Acknowledgment is a declaration of an individual who is described in the instrument and the one responsible for executing the written instrument.

Affiant is the individual who authors the affidavit and swears to the accuracy and truth of the statements made in the affidavit. The individual who takes an oath attesting that the contents are true and signs the statement is called an affiant

A Bill of sale is a written document that is given from the vendor to the vendee.

A certified copy is a copy of a public record signed and certified as true by a public official. A notary public has NO authority to issue certified copies. Notaries are not allowed to certify the authenticity of legal documents and other documents that are filed with foreign consular officers.

Chattel is a term to describe personal property like household items, cars, and fixtures. It does not include real estate.

Chattel paper is a document that gives evidence of both an obligation to pay money and a security interest in a lease or for specified goods. The agreement that provides for the security interest is known as the security agreement.

Codicil is an instrument created subsequent to a will and attached to the original will when some edits are required.

Cognomen is essentially a third personal name. This practice was common during the Roman era when citizens were given third names. The name is usually passed down from the father to the son.

Communication technology means an electronic process or device that permits the notary to communicate with a remotely located individual

Consideration is anything of value when entering a contract; it may involve personal services, money, or even affection.

Contempt of court is a term used to describe disrespectful behavior in court in front of a judge; it often leads to disruption of court proceedings.

A contract is a legal agreement between competent parties. It is usually in writing and clearly states what rights each party has.

Conveyance is a document in writing where real estate property is transferred, created, surrendered, or assigned.

A credential analysis is a service or a process operating according to developed standards through which a third party affirms the validity of government-issued ID through a review of public and proprietary data.

A credential service provider is a third party that registers and/or verifies subscriber authenticators; in addition, the service provider will issue electronic credentials to valid subscribers.

A Deponent is a person who takes an oath confirming that the written statement is true.

A deposition is a process where the testimony of a witness is taken out of court under oath or by affirmation before a notary public or a lawyer. The testimony authorized by law can be used at a trial or a hearing.

Duress is an unlawful constraint exercised on an

individual where he or she is forced to do some type of action against their will.

An electronic notarial act is an official and legal act performed by a notary public who is physically present in New York State. It may also involve maintaining an electronic record and only using communication technology that has been authorized.

An electronic notary public is a notary public who has registered with the Secretary of State and demonstrated the capability of performing electronic notarial acts according to the law.

Electronic record -information that is generated, created, communicated, sent, received, and stored by electronic means.

An electronic signature is any electronic signature affixed to an electronic notary in the performance of an electronic notarial act.

Escrow is the placement of an instrument in the hands of a third party. For example, when buying a home, the buyer will place funds in an escrow account; the person in charge of the escrow account will then deliver the money to the seller when all the conditions are met.

An Executor is a person named in a will who will carry out the provisions listed in the will. If no one is named in the will as an executor, then sometimes the probate court will appoint an executor.

Ex parte- is an examination or hearing in the presence of or on paper by one party/individual only/usually the other party is absent. For example, in restraining orders, one party may go to the judge to get the order, but the other party is absent.

A felony is a much more serious crime than a misdemeanor and is frequently punished by prolonged incarceration or even death.

Guardian is a person in charge of minors, property, or the person.

Identity proofing is a process whereby a credential service provider validates, collects, and verifies information about an individual.

Identity verification- use of an authentic process by which a notary validates the identity of the principal and other individuals present for the notarial act

Judgment is a court decree that declares that one individual is indebted to another or that one individual is either innocent or guilty of a crime.

Jurat is part of an affidavit where the notary certifies that it was sworn before him. But it is not the same as an affidavit.

Laches is negligence or delays in asserting one's legal rights.

A lease is a contract where one obtains possession or control of a property/motor vehicle for a defined amount of time.

Lien is a legal claim or right to a specific real estate property. The lien is released when the debt is paid.

Litigation is the act of bringing about a lawsuit.

A misdemeanor is any other crime other than a felony.

A mortgage on real property is a document in writing that has been duly executed and delivered. It will lead to the creation of a lien on a specific property for payment of a specified debt.

Notarial acts mean any official act that the notary is authorized to perform by law.

A notary public is an individual who meets the qualifications and is appointed by the Secretary of State to perform notarial acts according to the law.

Personal appearance means presence at a translation for which a notarial act is required, either electronically or physically, in a manner that meets all requirements.

A plaintiff is a person who initiates a suit or brings forth a lawsuit against another individual.

Power of attorney is a written statement by a person giving another individual the power to act on his or her behalf.

The proof is defined as a formal declaration that is usually made by a subscribing witness when executing an instrument. The witness usually states that he knows the individual described in the instrument and saw him execute the instrument.

Protest Is a formal statement written by the notary under seal that a certain payment or promissory note was presented and that such payment was refused.

Principal refers to the individual whose signature is reflected on a record that is notarized and 2) who has taken an oath or affirmation administered by the notary.

Public key infrastructure refers to organization, architecture, practices, techniques, and procedures that collectively support the operation of a certificate-based asymmetric or public key cryptographic system.

Seal is not required by all notaries. However, if it is used, it should identify the notary public, the jurisdiction of practice, and the authority. The only words that are required on the seal are the name of the notary public and the following "Notary Public For the State of New York.

Signature of notary: All notaries must sign their name; in addition, the notary must print, or stamp beneath his signature in BLACK ink, his name and the words, Notary Public State of New York, the name of the county where qualified, and the date when the commission expires

Statue: Law established by an act of the legislature

A statute of fraud is a law stating that in order to enforce certain contracts, there must be written evidence of the agreement/contract between the two parties

Statute of limitations: When an individual has been harmed by the negligent actions of another party, he or she only has a specific time within which to file a lawsuit- this time limit is known as the statute of limitations and may vary from one to three years, depending on the type of harm/injury.

Subordination clause: Clause that allows paying the mortgage at a later date which takes priority over the existing mortgage

Sunday: Notary can administer an oath or take an affidavit or acknowledgment on Sunday, but a deposition cannot be taken on Sunday in a civil proceeding

Swear: Mode authorized during administering of an oath.

Taking an acknowledgment; is an act of the individual named in the instrument who tells the notary that he is the individual named in the instrument and acknowledges that he executed the instrument. At the same time, this also involves the notary public obtaining satisfactory evidence of the person's identity.

Venue: Geographical place where the notary public takes the acknowledgment or affidavit. Venu must be listed on all notarized documents.

Will: Document that deals with the Disposition of one's estate after death.

Practice Test 1

1. The application fee for a notary commission in NYS is?

a. $20

b. $40

c. $60

d. $80

Answer C

All applicants have to submit a non-refundable fee of $60.

2. The term for a notary public in NYS is?

a. One-year

b. Two years

c. Four years

d. Five years

Answer C

A Notary public in NYS serves for four years and then needs to renew the commission.

3. Applicants who want to write the NYS notary exam have?

a. To sit the exam in Albany

b. The choice of visiting any testing center in the State

c. To make an appointment first

d. To first take a study course

Answer B

Tests for the NYS notary public exam are offered at many centers. It is on a first-come, first-serve basis.

4. In general, a notary public in NYS is commissioned to practice in what location?

a. Where they reside

b. Only in urban areas

c. In and out of State

d. Where the exam was taken

Answer A

Generally, a notary public is legally allowed to practice where he or she resides.

5. If an individual has been convicted of a misdemeanor, he can:

a. Only be a notary public if the misdemeanor was minor

b. Write to the Secretary of State to review his case

c. Become a notary public if the misdemeanor was more than five years ago

d. Become a notary public if he only has one misdemeanor

Answer B

While one cannot become a notary public if convicted of a felony. One may be able to with a misdemeanor. It all depends on the seriousness of the crime. Only the Secretary of State can make that determination.

6. When the county clerk issues a Certificate of Official Character (filing), what is the fee?

a. $2

b. $5

c. $7

d. $10

Answer D

The fee for issuing a Certificate of Official Character (filing) is $10. The fee for issuance is $5.

7. A notary public works for an insurance company. On the days he is off work, who can he delegate to continue with the notarizations?

a. Only his supervisor

b. Only his secretary

c. Anyone who works under him

d. No one

Answer D

The rule is that the notary public cannot delegate his responsibilities to any other person. It is illegal and can result in a loss of commission.

8. What is the name of the public officer who can administer oaths and acknowledgments just like a notary

public?

a. Mayor of the city

b. Commissioner of Deeds

c. Inspector general

d. Attorney general

Answer B

The Commissioner of Deeds is a public officer and can administer acknowledgments and oaths to citizens of NYS.

9. For a notary public to have his signature kept on file in multiple counties in the State, he has to first file for a:

a. Duplicate ID card

b. Certificate of character

c. Certificate of Commission

d. Seal

Answer B

The signature of a notary public is only kept on file in the county where he or she first registered. To have the signature on file in other counties, the notary public must first file for a Certificate of Character.

10. When a notary public submits a formal protest for non-payment, how much fee can he charge?

a. $0.75

b. $2

c. $5

d. $7

Answer A

The fee for a formal protest of nonpayment is 75 cents.

11. What is the maximum number of protest notices a notary public can submit for non-payment?

a. 2

b. 3

c. 4

d. 5

Answer 5

The notary public is only allowed to submit a maximum of 5 protest notices for nonpayment.

12. If a notary public forges a certificate, he may be guilty of a:

a. Misdemeanor

b. Felony

c. Infraction

d. Wilful neglect

Answer B

Forgery is a major crime leading to a charge of a felony; in addition, the penalty for a felony is much more severe than a misdemeanor.

13. What is the term called for a contract between a landlord and tenant that gives the latter the right to reside in the property for a fixed period of time?

a. Lease

b. Booking

c. Tenure

d. Residency

Answer A

A lease is a formal legal contract between a landlord and tenant; it gives the tenant permission to reside in the property for a specified period of time.

14. Which of the following is false about the duties of a notary public?

a. The notary public may administer an oath on a Sunday

b. The notary public may take an affidavit on a Sunday

c. The notary public may take an acknowledgment on a Sunday

d. The notary public may take a civil deposition on a Sunday

Answer D

The notary is not allowed to take a civil deposition on a Sunday but can perform other notarial acts.

15. What is the name of the instrument that ensures that one's assets will be distributed as stated after death?

a. Deed

b. Will

c. Pledge

d. Promise

Answer B

When a will is written, it ensures that the estate will be distributed according to the wishes of the decedent- the will overrides many legal provisions on how the estate should be distributed.

16. When a notary public has a pecuniary interest in a transaction, he or she:

a. Can continue to function as a notary public

b. Is not allowed to perform notarial acts

c. Should have a witness present during the sign-in process

d. Should consult with a lawyer

Answer B

In general, if a notary public has a pecuniary interest in a transaction, he or she should not perform any notarial act.

17. A new notary has been charged with making a forged seal. What punishment can he face?

a. Can have the commission revoked

b. Be charged in criminal court

c. Can be sued for damages in a civil court

d. All of the above

Answer D

Forgery is a serious crime and is associated with a range of penalties. In most cases, the notary public commission will be revoked, and the individual will be charged in criminal court. Any individual harmed as a result of this action can also sue the notary public in civil court.

18. At the end of the document, the Will maker has inserted a provision that clearly states the formalities which will make the asset distribution effective. What is this provision known as?

a. Last testament

b. Trust

c. Attestation clause

d. Affirmation clause

Answer C

At the end of a Will, some authors will insert a provision that states the formalities that will be needed to make the asset distribution effective and efficient. This is known as the Attestation clause.

19. In general, in New York State, who cannot issue

certificates involved with notary public functions?

a. The county clerk's office

b. The Mayor's office

c. The Secretary of State

d. A notary public

Answer B

The Mayor's office cannot electively perform notarial acts if there is no notary public on board.

20. A public employee walks into the office of the county clerk for an affidavit. What will be the cost of this undertaking?

a. Zero

b. $2

c. $4

d. $5

Answer A

During business hours, there is no fee for notarial acts at the county clerk's office.

21. When the applicant passes the notary exam and meets the eligibility criteria to become a notary, what is the total commission fee that has to be paid?

a. $20

b. $40

c. $60

d. $80

Answer C

The total commission fee to be paid after passing the exam is a non-refundable fee of $60.

22. Notaries are allowed to charge how much fee for swearing in a witness?

a. $2

b. $4

c. $7

d. $10

Answer A

For swearing in a witness, the notary public can charge no more than $2.

23. When a county clerk issues the Certificate of Official Character, the notary public will be charged?

a. $2

b. $4

c. $5

d. $7

Answer C

The county clerk has a set fee of $5 to issue a Certificate of Official Character.

24. What is the fee for notary public authentication?

a. $1

b. $2

c. $3

d. $4

Answer C

Authentication of a notary public costs $3. This means that the county clerk verifies the signature of the notary public.

25. What is the fee for renewal of a notary public commission?

a. $20

b. $40

c. $60

d. $80

Answer C

The set fee for renewal of commission is $60. The fee is non-refundable and has to be sent to the county clerk.

26. What is the fee for an authentication certificate?

a. $2

b. $3

c. $4

d. $6

Answer B

The fee for an authentication certificate is $3

27. A notary public shares office space with a college friend of his, who is a lawyer. How should the notary public function?

a. Offer legal advice only on matters that he knows well

b. Split the fees with his colleague

c. Can state that he has good knowledge of the law to his clients

d. Avoid the practice of law

Answer D

The best advice is for a notary public not to practice law or give out any legal advice. It is taboo to practice law without qualifications in NYS.

28. A notary public identification card _____:

a. Cannot be replaced when it is damaged

b. It cannot be replaced when it is lost

c. It is issued by the Secretary of State

d. Can be duplicated by the notary public

Answer C

The notary public identification card is usually issued by the Secretary of State. The card should not be duplicated by the notary public- this can only be done by the Secretary of State.

29. When a disbarred notary public continues to provide notarial services, he can be guilty of a:

a. Felony

b. Wilful neglect

c. Infraction

d. Misdemeanor

Answer D

After being disbarred, a notary public should cease working as a notary public. Doing so can lead to a misdemeanor.

30. Which of the following is a function of a notary public in NYS?

a. Prepare a mortgage document

b. Edit a will and attach a codicil

c. Officiate a funeral

d. None of the above

Answer D

A notary public is not allowed to do any of the above. In addition, the notary public should not pretend to practice law or even give out legal advice.

Practice Test 2

1. A client has asked you to notarize an affidavit; at the same time, you ask him to swear an oath. Which of the following is false?

a. The client must bring along a photo Identification

b. The instrument has to be signed in the presence of the notary

c. The notary public may ask the signer to swear an oath prior to signing

d. The fee for an oath is $20

Answer D

Citizens of New York State who want documents notarized need to bring the relevant documents and a photo. The sign-in must be done in the presence of the notary public. The fee for an oath is $2.

2. If a notary public consistently charges higher fees

than those recommended by the Secretary of State, he can be punished by:

a. 12 months incarceration

b. $500 fine

c. Treble damages to the person aggrieved

d. Loss of commission

Answer C

In general, if the notary public consistently charges higher fees than those set by the State, he may be punished, and this may include paying treble the damages if a person is harmed.

3. A new notary recently refused to notarize an affidavit. What is the possible penalty for this offense?

a. 1-month incarceration

b. Three months incarceration

c. Six months incarceration

d. 12 months incarceration

Answer D

Refusing to work as a public officer without a valid reason can result in a misdemeanor and up to 12 months of incarceration.

4. Which of the following is NOT true about an application for a notary public?

a. The applicant can be an illegal immigrant

b. The applicant must be a resident of NYS

c. The applicant can be a permanent resident

d. The applicant should have a place of business in NYS

Answer A

To apply for a notary public, one does not have to be a

US citizen but must be a resident of New York State. At the time of appointment, however, the notary public has to be a US citizen. Illegal immigrants cannot apply to become a notary public in NYS.

5. Which of the following statements is false?

a. Even after conviction of a misdemeanor, one can be appointed as notary public

b. Even after conviction of a felony, one can be appointed as notary public

c. A conviction for possession of illicit drugs usually means one cannot be appointed as a notary public

d. Prior conviction of prostitution prevents one from becoming a notary

Answer B

In general, once a person has been convicted of a felony, there is zero chance of becoming a notary public in NYS.

6. A notary public who moves out of State is deemed to be a resident of a New York County provided he:

a. Visits New York State every month

b. Has family who lives in New York State

c. Has a driver's license from New York State

d. Has a business office in New York State

Answer D

Even if a notary public moves out of State, as long as he or she maintains an office in NYS, he can practice as a notary public. Once the office is closed, then the notary term becomes invalid.

7. What is the fee for issuing a duplicate identification card?

a. $2

b. $5

c. $7

d. $10

Answer D

The fee for issuing a duplicate ID card is $10, which is the same fee for changing the address or name of a notary public.

8. What is the fee for writing the notary public exam?

a. $20

b. $15

c. $10

d. $25

Answer B

The fee for writing the notary public exam is $15.

9. What does the county clerk charge to issue a certificate of a notarial signature?

a. $1

b. $3

c. $5

d. $7

Answer B

Certification of a notarial signature that is issued by the county clerk will cost $3

10. Once an individual is removed as a notary public by the Secretary of State, is he or she eligible for reappointment in the future?

a. No

b. Yes

c. Only after review by the county clerk

d. Only after a review by the Secretary of State

Answer A

In general, once a notary public has been removed from office, he/she is not eligible for reappointment.

11. Which of the following is a false statement?

a. The county clerk may select one individual in the office who will notarize documents

b. The notarization done by the office worker will be free of charge

c. The person selected by the county clerk will need to pay a fee for the notary exam

d. The person selected by the county clerk will not have to pay an application fee

Answer C

The county clerk may select one individual from the office to notarize documents for the public free of charge. That individual is usually exempt from the application fee and the notary exam fee.

12. The seal and signature of the county clerk on a certificate of official character may be:

a. Printed

b. Photographed

c. Stamped

d. All of the above

Answer D

The signature and seal of the county clerk on a certificate of official character or authentication may be printed, facsimile, stamped, or even photographed.

13. When a notary public commits fraud with intent to

harm others, he or she is:

a. Not liable for damages to others

b. Is liable for damages to others as a result of his actions

c. Is immune from litigation

d. Is protected by the Secretary of State

Answer B

A notary public is liable to all parties that may be injured or suffer damages as a result of his or her actions.

14. When an ordinary individual pretends to act as a notary public, he or she can be guilty of a:

a. Felony

b. Misdemeanor

c. Infraction

d. Wilful neglect

Answer B

An individual not commissioned as a notary public but acts as one can be guilty of a misdemeanor.

15. After opening a safe deposit box, within how many days must a copy of the notary public's certificate be mailed to the lessee?

a. Three days

b. Five days

c. Seven days

d. Ten days

Answer D

After a safe deposit box is opened in the presence of a notary public, the lessee should be mailed the certificate within ten days.

16. After sending a notice to the lessee about an expired safe deposit box, when can the bank (lessor) open the safe box?

a. After five days

b. After ten days

c. After 15 days

d. After 30 days

Answer D

The expired safe deposit box can only be opened 30 days after the notice is mailed to the lessee.

17. For a class D felony, the incarceration period is?

a. Not more than one year

b. Not more than two years

c. Not more than seven years

d. Not more than ten years

Answer C

For a class D felony, the courts usually do not incarcerate people for more than seven years.

18. If a notary is guilty of a class A misdemeanor, how long will his incarceration be?

a. Not more than one-month

b. Not more than three months

c. Not more than six months

d. Not more than 12 months

Answer D

For a class A misdemeanor, imprisonment is usually not more than 12 months.

19. When a notary public alters or falsely makes a written instrument, he can be charged with what degree of forgery?

a. First

b. Second

c. Third

d. Fourth

Answer B

Altering or falsely making a written instrument can result in a charge of second-degree forgery.

20. A notary public agrees to take an acknowledgment of a distant friend over the phone. This can result in what criminal charge?

a. Felony

b. misdemeanor

c. Infraction

d. Wilful neglect

Answer B

Taking an acknowledgment over the phone is not permitted and can lead to a misdemeanor charge.

21. If a disbarred notary public continues to function as a notary public and executes all types of instruments, he can be guilty of:

a. Wilful negligence

b. Felony

c. Misdemeanor

d. Infraction

Answer C

Once removed or barred from office, working as a notary public is illegal and can result in a charge of a misdemeanor.

22. Which one of the following is not eligible for the office of a notary public?

a. Commissioner of elections

b. Sheriff

c. Member of the legislature

d. Inspector of elections

Answer B

A Sheriff is not eligible for the office of a notary public.

23. A written law passed by a legislative body is known as a?

a. Statute

b. Attestation

c. Affirmation

d. Jurat

Answer A

When a legislative body passes a written law, this is known as a statute.

24. In general, a notary public in NYS can:

a. Officiate a wedding

b. Witness and certify the marriage

c. Only solemnize the wedding if both parties are known to the notary public

d. Cannot legally officiate a wedding ceremony

Answer D

In general, a notary public cannot officiate a wedding

ceremony.

25. In NYS, the notary public fee for an oath or affirmation is:

a. $2

b. $5

c. $7

d. $10

Answer A

The notary public fee for an oath or affirmation is $2.

26. When the county clerk issues a Certificate of Official Character to a notary public, the seal and signature may be:

a. Printed

b. Facsimile

c. Stamped

d. All of the above

Answer D

The seal and signature on the Certificate of Official character can be printed, stamped, or facsimile.

27. Which of the following about oaths and affirmations by a NYS notary public is false?

a. The notary public is permitted to administer an oath to himself

b. The notary public can administer an affirmation

c. The notary public can certify an affirmation

d. The notary public can receive an acknowledgment

Answer A

The notary public is not permitted to administer an oath to himself.

28. Any individual who claims to be a notary public, when in reality he is not, can be guilty of a:

a. Felony

b. Misdemeanor

c. Infraction

d. Wilful negligence

Answer B

Claiming to be a notary public when in reality, one is not is illegal and can result in a misdemeanor.

29. The act of transferring property from one party to another using a legal document is known as:

a. Reconveyance

b. Conveyance

c. Auction

d. Transference

Answer B

Conveyance is a legal term that refers to the act of transferring real estate property from one party to another. The document will usually state the date of actual transfer, agreed upon price as well as the responsibilities and obligations of both parties.

30. A notary public who has been charged with fraudulent practice takes the acknowledgment or proof of a conveyance. According to the law, he is:

a. Guilty of a petty offense

b. Not liable if no harm results

c. Liable for damages to the person injured

d. Only guilty if the instrument is invalid

Answer C

In general, if a notary public has been charged with any type of crime, he or she can be liable for any damages if there is harm to the person involved.

Practice Test 3

1. When a bank (Lessor) opens a safe deposit box in the presence of a notary public, the latter is supposed to:

a. Take an inventory

b. Take the assets and place them in an escrow account

c. Call the depositor and tell him what he found

d. Determine the cash value of the items

Answer A

In general, the notary is supposed to make an inventory of the items found in the safe deposit box. The document should list the date, name of the bank, and type of items found.

2. What is the name of the law that is a consolidation of New York State laws that govern legal procedures in the Unified Court system, such as a deposition before a notary public?

a. Civil practice law and rules

b. Contract Law

c. New York Tort law

d. Field code

Answer A

The New York Civil Practice Law and Rules (CPLR) is a vast collection of the Laws of New York; the CPLR reveals the legal process in the US courts, such as jurisdiction, venue and pleadings. Further, the CPLR also contains provisions for the statute of limitations and the different liabilities.

3. The rule which authorizes a deposition to be taken before a notary public in a civil proceeding is found in the following:

a. Criminal Procedure Law

b. NYS Administrative Code

c. Family Court Act

d. Civil Practice Law and Rules

Answer D

The rule that allows for depositions to be taken can be found in the Civil Practice Law and Rules document.

4. Which of the following statements about notary public is false?

a. A notary public can give an oath to any citizen

b. A notary public is not allowed to prepare a Will

c. A notary public can only offer a legal opinion but not practice law

d. A notary public usually should not charge fees for notarial acts for military personnel

Answer C

A notary public must not practice law if he or she has

not had formal legal education. It is illegal to practice as a lawyer when one does not have the education and training.

5. If a notary public asks for higher fees than those stated by the Secretary of State, what type of penalty can he or she face?

a. Loss of commission

b. Civil lawsuit

c. Criminal prosecution

d. All of the above

Answer D

When a notary public charges higher fees than those stated by the Secretary of State, he can face a number of punishments, including loss of commission, criminal prosecution, and/or a civil lawsuit.

6. After advertising as a lawyer, when a notary public was not one, he was penalized with a Class A misdemeanor. In general, if the penalty is incarceration, what will be the duration?

a. One month

b. No more than a year

c. At least two years

d. Usually less than 48-72 hours

Answer B

In all cases, being charged with a misdemeanor will not result in prolonged incarceration. The maximum time in prison is usually no more than 12 months.

7. A 78-year-old has just made a Will and appointed a person to carry out the wishes stated in the Will. This person is known as a:

a. Beneficiary

b. Grantor

c. Trustee

d. Executor

Answer D

When making a will, the person appointed to carry out the wishes of the will-maker is known as the Executor.

8. A 69-year-old dies in a motor vehicle accident but had no will. His estate goes to the probate court, where a person is appointed to manage the estate. This individual is known as the:

a. Beneficiary

b. Trustee

c. Trustor

d. Executor

Answer D

In the absence of a will, the probate court will usually appoint a person to manage the assets. This individual is known as an executor or a personal representative.

9. What is the name of the individual who signs the affidavit and swears to the accuracy of the statements made in the document?

a. Executor

b. Lessee

c. Affiant

d. Notary public

Answer C

An affiant is an individual who is the author of an affidavit. This individual first swears to the accuracy and truth of the statements made in the affidavit.

10. A document that can change or alter the provisions

in a Will and be attached to the Will is known as a:

a. Affirmation

b. Codicil

c. Contract

d. Title

Answer B

In general, one is not permitted to make major changes to a will if errors are spotted or the Will needs an upgrade. In such scenarios, one can add a codicil. A codicil allows for any change, alteration, or deletion to the provisions listed in the Will. The codicil is then attached to the Will- it has to be signed and dated.

11. What is the term for tangible property that is moveable between locations?

a. Chattel

b. Assets

c. Income

d. Accessories

Answer A

Chattel refers to tangible items that can be moved and may include furniture, cars, hogs, etc. It does not include real estate property.

12. A 38-year-old was refused notary services by a notary for no apparent reason. He then initiated a civil lawsuit. In the lawsuit, he will be named as the:

a. Defendant

b. Beneficiary

c. Plaintiff

d. Appellant

Answer C

The person filing the lawsuit is usually called a

plaintiff.

13. A notary public was found guilty of a misdemeanor. Now he wants to appeal the decision to a higher court. He will be defined as the:

a. Plaintiff

b. Defendant

c. Beneficiary

d. Appellant

Answer D

An appellant is an individual who appeals to the judgment of a lower court to a higher court. In most cases, the appellant is not happy with the lower court's ruling.

14. What is the name of the law that sets the maximum amount of time that the parties involved in a dispute have to initiate legal proceedings?

a. Statute of Limitations

b. Ultimate Limitation Period

c. The Dispute law

d. The Fraud law

Answer A

The statute of limitations is a legal doctrine that sets the time to initiate legal proceedings. When two parties are in dispute, they only have a defined time period within which to initiate a lawsuit from the date of the alleged crime/offense. The length of time allowed by the statute varies from 1-3 years.

15. The notary public usually provides notarial services at?

a. City Hall

b. The Mayor's office

c. A venue

d. The County Clerk's office

Answer C

The immediate location where the notary public provides services is called the venue.

16. What is the name of the document certified by the Minister of Foreign Affairs that can be used in another country?

a. Apostille

b. Certificate

c. Deed

d. Credential

Answer A

Apostille is a document usually certified by the Consular services for international use. For example, credentials and certificates from foreign countries often have to be certified by the Minister of Foreign Affairs.

17. The fee charged by the county clerk to verify the signature of a notary public is:

a. $3

b. $5

c. $7

d. $10

Answer A

To verify if the signature of the notary public is authentic, the fee charged by the county clerk is $3.

18. An individual makes an unreasonable delay in making a claim in court that results in a refusal; this is known as

a. Lazy

b. Laches

c. Imprudent

d. Tardy

Answer B

Laches usually means an unreasonable delay in making an assertion or claim in court. For example, many cases are thrown out of court because plaintiffs make unreasonable delays in making their claims.

19. What is the meaning of the word 'attests?'

a. Confirm

b. Witness

c. Promise

d. Certify

Answer B

The term attests means to witness. One can witness the execution of a written document at the request of the individual who authored the document.

20. What is the name of the term when the document legally transfers property ownership from the seller to the buyer?

a. Deed

b. Bill of Sale

c. Invoice

d. Title

Answer B

The Bill of Sale is a document that transfers ownership of property or any item from the seller to the buyer. It acts as a sales receipt.

21. What is it called when an individual provides testimony out of court under oath before an officer; this testimony may be used at a trial.

a. Deposition

b. Disposition

c. Sublimation

d. Evidence

Answer A

The act of deposition usually involves providing testimony out of court in front of a notary public, lawyer, or public officer. The individual has to first take an oath, and the proceedings are recorded and can be used later in court or at a hearing.

22. The individual who establishes a trust fund is known as a:

a. Grantee

b. Grantor

c. Beneficiary

d. Recipient

Answer B

The creator of the trust fund is known as the grantor. The trust allows for the legal transfer of assets to the trustee, who will distribute the assets according to the wishes of the grantor.

23. In general, chattel does not refer to:

a. Furniture

b. Hogs

c. Automobiles

d. Homes

Answer D

Chattel is a catch-all term to describe property that can be moved. It may refer to either animate or inanimate properties such as furniture, hogs, and automobiles. It never includes real estate.

24. When there is a motion in court for an order to be granted without waiting for a response from the other party, this is known as

a. Guilt by association

b. Ex parte

c. Premature judgment

d. In vivo

Answer B

Sometimes, in civil proceedings, motions for orders are granted without waiting to get a response from the other party. Generally, these situations involve temporary restraining orders. This is known as ex parte.

25. What type of crime is punishable by a prison sentence that is usually more than a year?

a. Misdemeanor

b. Wilful neglect

c. Felony

d. Infraction

Answer C

In most felony cases, the prison sentence is over a year. With a misdemeanor, the sentence is usually less than a year.

26. What is the term called when an individual is unlawfully constrained and forced to do something against his wishes?

a. Pressure

b. Duress

c. Compulsion

d. Force

Answer B

Duress is defined as an unlawful constraint that is exercised on an individual whereby he or she is then forced to do an activity against his wishes.

27. When the Secretary of State issues a Certificate of Official Character, what fee will be collected?

a. $2

b. $5

c. $7

d. $10

Answer D

When the Secretary of State issues a Certificate of Official Character, the fee is $10.

28. During business hours, each county clerk can designate how many members of their staff to act as a notary public to notarize documents?

a. One

b. Two

c. Three

d. A minimum of 5

Answer A

The county clerk may select One member of the staff to notarize public documents during business hours. There is usually no fee for this service during business hours.

29. Following the death of both parents, the two minor children were looked after by another adult. This person is usually known as a:

a. Guardian

b. Adoptee

c. Adoptor

d. Stepfather

Answer A

A guardian is usually an individual who is in charge of a minor's property or looks after the minor.

30. What is the term called when a bank or lender has placed a legal claim against a property for an unpaid mortgage?

a. Lien

b. Outstanding Bill

c. Security

d. Encumbrance

Answer A

A lien is a legal claim against a property; it is usually placed by a creditor for unpaid bills. Liens are commonly placed against homes and cars until the owner pays up. If the debt is unpaid, the property can be auctioned, or the home can be foreclosed.

Practice Test 4

1. What is it called when an individual provides a written statement that he is giving another person the power to act on his behalf?

a. Will

b. Trust

c. Power of attorney

d. Guardianship

Answer C

A power of attorney is a legal document that gives an individual permission to act on behalf of the author.

2. What is the term called when a notary public makes a formal statement that a certain bill of exchange for payment on a certain date was refused?

a. Rejection

b. Outstanding

c. Overdue

d. Protest

Answer D

A protest is a formal statement in writing by the notary public. It is usually written when a certain bill or promissory note on a specified date is presented and is either accepted or refused.

3. When a notary public places his signature on an instrument, what else is required?

a. Has to sign with black ink

b. Must write the terms 'Notary Public State of New York.'

c. Must name the county where registered

d. All of the above

Answer D

A notary public must sign the name under which he or she was appointed. In addition to the venue and signature, the notary public may stamp or print his signature in black ink. The terms "Notary Public State of New York" must be written, including when the commission expires and the name of the county where qualified.

4. What is the term in a recent real estate deal that places priority over which mortgage has to be paid off first?

a. Subordination clause

b. Obligation clause

c. Financing clause

d. Title clause

Answer A

A Subordination clause in real estate gives preference to one loan repayment over the other. This usually occurs when the individual has two mortgages. The priority loan has to be paid off first.

5. What are the education requirements for becoming a notary public in NYS?

a. Must be a college grad

b. Must have at least a bachelor's degree

c. Must at least have a college diploma

d. Have common school education

Answer D

NY law says that to become a notary public, one only needs a common school education. There are no requirements for a college degree or a diploma.

6. A notary public working out of Brooklyn moves to

neighboring New Jersey but still maintains a place of business in NYS. What is his status as a notary public?

a. Once he moves out of state, he is not allowed to practice as a notary public

b. As long as he maintains a place of business in NY state, he can continue to work as a notary public

c. He can work as a notary in New Jersey with a commission from NYS

d. He can ask his clients to come to New Jersey for notarization

Answer B

Even if a notary public moves out of state, he can still work as a notary public as long as he maintains a business office in NYS. Once the business office is vacated, he is no longer able to work as a notary public in the state.

7. What is the current status of taking

acknowledgments over the phone in NYS?

a. Allowed

b. Not allowed

c. Only allowed if the phone line is secured

d. Only allowed if the phone is first registered with the county clerk

Answer B

No notarial act can be carried out over the phone. It is not permitted.

8. What is the fee for re-appointment as a notary public?

a. $10

b. $20

c. $40

d. $60

Answer D

The fee for re-appointment as a notary public is $60, which is non-refundable

9. For renewal of the notary commission, the application has to be sent to the following:

a. Secretary of state

b. County clerk

c. Both the county clerk and Secretary of State

d. None of the above

Answer B

For renewals, the application needs to be sent to the county clerk where the notary public first registered. Note when first applying to become a notary public, the application is submitted to the Secretary of State.

10. What is the fee for a name change of a notary public?

a. $2

b. $4

c. $7

d. $10

Answer D

The fee for name or address change is $10. However, if the name and address change is made during the renewal period, there is no need to pay the extra $10.

11. When a notary ID card is replaced, what words will it usually bear?

a. Duplicate

b. Pending approval

c. Approved

d. Valid

Answer A

A replacement ID card will have the term DUPLICATE written over it.

12. What is the fee to replace an ID card?

a. $2

b. $5

c. $7

d. $10

Answer D

Replacement of a damaged, stolen, or lost ID card will cost $10.

13. When a notary public gets married and changes her name, what is the protocol for notarization?

a. Should start using the married name on all notarizations

b. Should only use the name on the original commission for notarization

c. Can use either name for notarization

d. Should add the married name in parenthesis during the notarization

Answer D

When a notary public gets married, she can add her new name (in parenthesis) immediately. When it is time for the renewal of the commission, she can decide which name she would like to use-but; she can't use both names.

14. Prior to a jurat, the signer must?

a. Present at least two photo IDs

b. Take an oath

c. Have two witnesses verify his/her identity

d. Pay a sum of $25 to the notary public

Answer B

Prior to a jurat, all individuals must take an oath, to tell the truth. The oath is taken before signing the instrument.

15. Which of the following is a true statement about working as a notary public in the county clerk's office?

a. The county clerk usually selects at least two people from the office to work as notary public

b. The person selected to work as a notary public has to offer weekend services

c. The person selected to work as a notary public should be available during business hours

d. The person selected to work as a notary public can

only charge $2 for the notarial service

Answer C

The county clerk will usually select one individual from the office to work as a notary public. This person must be available during business hours, and the cost of notarization is free.

16. A newly commissioned notary public has been charged with a felony, and the Secretary of State has sought his removal. Prior to this undertaking, what should be done?

a. Ask the notary to seek legal counsel

b. Have a Zoom call with the notary to hear his side

c. Send him a copy of the charges

d. Repeat a background check

Answer C

When a notary public is charged with any type of

crime, prior to removal, the laws dictate that he or she should be first sent a copy of the charges.

17. In general, the notary public identification card does not contain which of the following information?

a. The address of the notary public

b. The name of the notary public

c. The term length of the commission

d. The date when the commission started

Answer D

The notary public identification card contains the address, appointee's name, commission term, and county of practice.

18. In general, who is responsible for issuing reappointment commissions to the notary public in NYS?

a. The Secretary of State

b. The county clerk

c. The mayor's office

d. The National Association of Notaries

Answer B

Reappointments are usually done by the county clerk where the notary was already in practice. However, remember the initial application to become a notary public goes to the Secretary of State.

19. When a notary public applies for reappointment, he or she submits a fee of $60. How much of this fee is then transmitted to the Secretary of State by the county clerk?

a. $10

b. $20

c. $30

d. $40

Answer D

After receiving a total of $60 for the reapplication, the county clerk will send $40 to the Secretary of State.

20. When a notary public makes a name or address change, he has to send in a non-refundable fee of how many dollars to the Secretary of State?

a. $2

b. $5

c. $7

d. $10

Answer D

The fee for name or address change is $10, and it is non-refundable.

21. An individual who has been appointed by the court to manage the estate of an individual who died without a will is known as the:

a. Beneficiary

b. Trustee

c. Grantor

d. Administrator

Answer D

If a person dies without a will, then the estate goes to probate. The court will then select an administrator to manage the estate. Probate is a long and expensive affair. In some texts, the administrator is also referred to as the executor of the Will.

22. To avoid having to requalify as a notary public, within what time period after the expiration of the present term must he or she apply for renewal?

a. Within one-month

b. Within two months

c. Within four months

d. Within 6 months

Answer D

A notary public has to apply within six months after expiration in order to avoid going through the entire application again.

23. In general, a notary public who is enlisted in the military is given how much time to reapply after the term of his present commission expires?

a. Three months

b. Six months

c. Nine months

d. 12 months

Answer D

Notary publics who are enlisted in the military are usually given 12 months to reapply after the end of their term after leaving the military. It must be an honorable discharge, however.

24. When a notary public is charged with misconduct, he can be suspended by the Secretary of State. But what must precede this action?

a. The notary public should speak to a lawyer

b. The notary public should ask for a copy of the charges

c. The notary public should speak to the county clerk

d. The notary public should initiate legal action against the Secretary of State

Answer B

Before the notary public can be suspended after being

charged with misconduct, he or she must be given a copy of the charges so that he can prepare a defense.

25. When a notary public wants a duplicate identification card, what is the fee for this service from the Secretary of State will cost?

a. $2

b. $5

c. $7

d. $10

Answer D

The fee for a duplicate ID card is $10.

26. What is the name of the document that certifies the commission of a notary public in a different county?

a. Certificate of Authenticity

b. Certificate of Character

c. New York State Notary public

d. Certificate of Commission

Answer B

A Certificate of Character is first needed before one can work in another county.

27. Recently a notary public was removed from office because of perjury. When can he reapply for the same position?

a. Only after seven years

b. After retaking the exam in 2 years

c. Never

d. After submitting letters of support to the Secretary of State

Answer C

Once a notary public has been removed from office, it is impossible to get reinstated. The removal is permanent.

28. A notary public was recently removed from office but yet executed an instrument as a notary public for a close friend. He may be guilty of a?

a. Felony

b. Misdemeanor

c. Wilful neglect

d. Infraction

Answer B

Signing or executing any instruments once the notary commission is not valid is a crime. One can be charged with a misdemeanor.

29. A notary public in NYS has been asked by a friend living in Connecticut to notarize his documents. What is

the current status of out-of-state notarizations?

a. The notary public can travel to Connecticut to perform the notarization

b. The notary public is only allowed to notarize documents within NYS

c. The notary public can ask for temporary permission from the county clerk to notarize documents out of state. A NYS notary public can notarize documents if he has an office in Connecticut

Answer B

Under New York Law, a notary public is only permitted to notarize documents in New York- there are no exceptions.

30. When a notary public is appointed in NYS, what item will he receive the following from the county clerk?

a. A notary seal

b. A booklet to record notarial acts

c. An official ID card

d. A rubber stamp

Answer C

When appointed as a notary public, the county clerk will send the individual an official ID card.

Practice Test 5

1. A 77-year-old recently died with no will, and his estate has gone to the probate court, which will appoint a person to manage the estate. What is the name of this person?

a. Beneficiary

b. Trustee

c. Administrator

d. Grantor

Answer C

When a person dies without a will, the probate court will usually appoint a person to manage the estate. This person is known as the administrator. He may be part of the family or have no relations to the family.

2. What is the term called when the Minister of Foreign Affairs confirms that the documents have been obtained

legally and issues a Specialized certificate?

a. Affidavit

b. Apostille

c. Chapeau

d. Amendment

Answer B

An apostille refers to a specialized certificate that is usually issued by the foreign ministry or consular service. The apostille confirms that the documents have been obtained in a legal manner- allowing them to be recognized in other nations.

3. What is the term called when there is a provision at the end of a Will that has been signed by a witness and states the manner of execution of the instrument?

a. Testament

b. Attestation clause

c. Solemn vow

d. Probate

Answer B

Some wills have an attestation clause which is a provision at the end of the document. The witness will usually certify that the instrument was executed before him and the manner of execution.

4. What is the term called when someone is allowed to make a solemn declaration because he or she conscientiously objects to taking an oath?

a. Addendum

b. Affirmation

c. Refutation

d. Denial

Answer B

In law, some people may not want to take the oath for a variety of reasons. These individuals can then make a solemn declaration when they conscientiously object to taking the oath.

5. What is the name of the document that reveals both a security interest and a monetary obligation in certain goods?

a. Bill of Sale

b. Chattel paper

c. IOU

d. Contract

Answer B

Chattel paper refers to a document that is utilized in secured transactions to sell property on credit while at the same time still retaining some interest in the property. The chattel paper has to show 1) a monetary obligation from one individual to another and 2) a secured interest retained in the property.

6. The supplementary document that allows you to make edits to the Will and attach it to the Will is known as the:

a. Papier

b. Deed

c. Last testament

d. Codicil

Answer D

The codicil is a legal document that acts as a supplement to the Will. Since one is not allowed to make major changes to the written Will, one can make a supplementary copy with the edits and attach it to the Will.

7. When something of value is given to induce another

person to enter into a contract, this is known as:

a. Enticement

b. Seduction

c. Consideration

d. Entrapment

Answer C

Consideration is the term used to describe when something of value is offered to another person so that he or she will enter into a contract. It is a common tactic when selling homes, cars, furniture, or even offering a job.

8. During a court session, the notary public got into a heated argument with the judge and showed disrespect to the court protocol. This type of behavior is known as:

a. Contempt of court

b. Guilt

c. Anger issues

d. Narcissistic

Answer A

When an individual shouts or fails to respect or listen to the judge or other people in the court, this is considered to be Contempt of court. Some people may refuse to cooperate with the judge or may exhibit threatening behavior.

9. What is the term called when there is a legal transfer of property ownership from one individual to another?

a. Conveyance

b. Deed

c. Title

d. Transfer

Answer A

Conveyance is the legal term used to describe the transfer of ownership of the title from the seller to the buyer. To be legally effective, conveyance must be documented in writing and signed by the individual who is selling or transferring the real estate property.

10. What is it called when an individual makes a formal statement outside the court but in the presence of a lawyer and promises to tell the truth?

a. Disposition

b. Deposition

c. Description

d. Distribution

Answer B

A deposition is a formal statement that an individual makes out of the courtroom to a notary or a public officer. First, he or she has to take an oath, and the statements are recorded to be used later in court or at a hearing.

11. What is the term called when funds are placed into the hands of a third party as a depository until the contract demands by both parties have been met?

a. Advanced banking

b. Investment

c. Escrow

d. Safe deposit box

Answer C

Escrow accounts are very common in real estate and law. Essentially when two parties are making a transaction, one party will place the funds in the hands of a third party (escrow). When the demands of both parties are met, the escrow funds will be released. For example, when a homebuyer will place funds in an escrow account with the stipulation that the money only be given to the seller once the home repairs have been made. When the home repairs are made, the escrow funds will be released to the seller, provided that the buyer is happy with the repairs.

12. In general, what is the true statement about attorneys and the notary public exam?

a. All attorneys need to take the exam

b. Attorneys do not need to take the exam

c. Only attorneys with a GPA below 3.2 need to take the exam

d. Attorneys only need to take the oral exam

Answer B

In general, a licensed and registered attorney in NYS does not have to take the notary exam to perform notarial duties.

13. In general, applicants for a notary public in New York State must have a minimum of what type of education?

a. Bachelor's degree

b. Technical diploma

c. Common school education

d. Be eligible to enter a college or university

Answer C

There are no strict education requirements to become a notary public in NYS. The law only requires that the applicant have common school education.

14. The Secretary of State states that some notary public administer oaths in a 'slipshod' manner. What is the meaning of Slipshod?

a. Neat and organized

b. Chronological manner

c. Hurried

d. Careless and sloppy

Answer D

Slipshod means careless and sloppy.

15. In which of the following cases can a notary public authenticate an instrument for a business?

a. Only if he is a manager

b. If he is only a stockholder

c. If he is the director

d. None of the above

Answer D

In general, if a notary public holds any type of position in a business that includes a director, employee, or stockholder, he is not permitted to authenticate any instrument. There could be a conflict of interest.

16. Which of the following errors can lead to the

invalidity of a notarized instrument?

a. If the notary public is working outside his jurisdiction

b. Misspelling the name of the notary public

c. Working with an expired term of commission

d. All of the above

Answer D

Some unintentional errors that can lead to the invalidity of a notarized document include jurisdiction issues, misspellings, expired term, having no business address, and ineligibility.

17. A bank has decided to open the safe deposit box that is past due. What is the current protocol required of a notary public at this event?

a. The notary public can be virtual

b. The notary public must physically be present

c. The notary public can send an assistant

d. The notary public can watch the proceedings on video

Answer B

When a bank opens a safe deposit box, the notary public must physically be present to take the inventory and document the items, the date, and the name of the bank.

18. To avoid retaking the exam, when should the notary public renew the license after it has expired?

a. 30 days

b. 60 days

c. Four months

d. Six months

Answer D

NYS offers a significant amount of time after the commission term has expired for license renewal. If the renewal is done within six months of expiration, there is no need to retake the exam.

19. Which of the following best describes a venue?

a. The county where the notary first registered

b. The city where the notary resides

c. The place where the notary public performs notarial acts

d. The location listed on the ID card

Answer C

The venue is best described as the county/place where the notary public performs notarial acts.

20. While in a hurry, a notary public forgets to add his ID number to the instrument during the notarization act.

Will this result in an invalid instrument?

a. Yes

b. No

c. Will have to redo the entire notarization again

d. Will need to speak to the county clerk

Answer B

In general, if there are minor errors during the notarial act, this does not mean that the instrument will be invalid. Errors are common, and as long as they are minor, they won't affect the validity of the instrument.

21. What is the civil penalty when a Notary public who is not an attorney gives legal advice?

a. $250

b. $500

c. $1,000

d. $5,000

Answer C

The civil penalty for giving legal advice as a notary public is $1,000.

22. When a public employee presents at the county clerk's office for notarization, what fee will he need to pay for taking an oath?

a. $1

b. $2

c. $4

d. Nothing

Answer D

In general, public employees who want to get documents notarized at the county clerk's office are not charged any fee for notarial acts.

23. Which statement is true about an attorney in NYS?

a. All attorneys need to pass the notary exam first

b. If licensed as a lawyer, can practice as a notary public

c. A Lawyer cannot be a notary public at the same time

d. Lawyers need to be commissioned by the Secretary of State to work as a notary public

Answer B

As long as a lawyer is licensed and registered, he or she can offer the same notarial services as a notary public.

24. Which of the following will appear on a notary public's identification card?

a. Name of appointee

b. County where registered

c. Commission term

d. All of the above

Answer D

The Notary public ID card will contain the name, address, commission term, and county where the individual is registered.

25. When a notary public violates the fee rules, the plaintiff may get?

a. $500 in compensation

b. Double the damages

c. Triple the damages

d. Reimbursement of his fee plus $1,000

Answer C

When a notary public violates the fee rules, plaintiffs can be awarded triple the damages if there is any resulting damage.

26. In general, a notary public should not:

a. Give advice on legal matters

b. Not ask for legal referrals

c. Not advertise that he or she is a legal professional

d. All of the above

Answer D

When it comes to the practice of law, the best advice for notary publics is to avoid the subject. Advice or opinion on legal matters is also not permitted. The state takes it very seriously when notary publics pretend to act like lawyers.

27. In general, a notary public should never acknowledge which document?

a. Passport application

b. Loan document

c. Rental application

d. Will

Answer D

The general rule is that a notary public should never acknowledge a will. This is best left to the lawyers.

28. What fee does the county clerk charge for the certification of a notarial signature?

a. $2

b. $3

c. $5

d. $7

Answer B

Certification of a notarial signature costs $3.

29. When a county clerk issues an authentication certificate, what process has he or she just completed?

a. Verified the address

b. Verified the notary public signature

c. Verified the county of practice

d. Verified the photo ID

Answer B

When the county clerk issues an authentication certificate, in essence, he or she has simply verified the notary public's signature.

30. What is it called when an individual delays asserting his rights in court?

a. Lackey

b. Larches

c. Lamey

d. Lackadaisical

Answer B

When one delays asserting his or her right in court, this is known as larches.

Practice Test 6

1. What is the term called when the notary public certifies that a part of an affidavit was sworn to him on a particular day?

a. Oath

b. Jurat

c. Depodent

d. Allegiance

Answer B

Part of an affidavit where the notary public certifies that it was sworn to before him (sworn before me on ... day of ...) is called the Jurat.

2. When a notary public wants a certificate of official character to be issued, the county clerk will charge a fee of?

a. $1

b. $2

c. $3

d. $5

Answer A

The fee charged by the county clerk for issuing a certificate of official character is $5. To file the certificate costs $10.

3. The final approval for the appointment of a notary public in NYS is made by?

a. Mayor

b. City Council

c. Secretary of State

d. County Clerk

Answer C

The final decision for approval of an application for a notary public is made by the Secretary of State.

4. When a person marries and wants to change her name, what is the fee at the time of the renewal of the commission?

a. No fee

b. $20

c. $30

d. $10

Answer A

If the person who gets married wants to change the name on the ID, then it is best to do it at the time of the renewal process. At this stage, there is no fee.

5. A public employee goes to the county clerk's office for an affidavit during office hours. What fee will he be charged?

a. $2

b. No charge

c. $5

d. $0.75 cents

Answer B

During office hours, many notarial services provided by the county clerk's office are FREE.

6. A newly commissioned notary public refused to officiate an oath for a client for no apparent reason. This refusal can result in what type of crime?

a. Felony

b. Misdemeanor

c. Infraction

d. Wilful negligence

Answer B

Refusing to provide notarial services for no reason can result in a misdemeanor.

7. What is the term called for the legal concept that recommends that certain types of contracts must be executed in writing in order to be valid?

a. Statute of Limitations

b. Statute of Fraud

c. Fraud legislation

d. Consumer protection legislation

Answer A

The statute of fraud is legal terminology which states that in order for certain contracts to be valid, they must be executed in writing. The prime reason for this is to avoid fraud.

8. What is the true statement about the use of notary seals in NYS?

a. All notaries must have a seal

b. Seals are not required by a notary public in NYS

c. The seal is mandatory for affidavits

d. The seal must be obtained from the Secretary of State

Answer B

Unlike many other states, in NYS, a seal is not mandatory for a notary public. A rubber stamp will do.

9. What is the name of the certificate that is usually issued by the State Department that permits international usage of the documents?

a. Visa

b. Apostille

c. Passport

d. Permit

Answer B

An apostille is a certificate that is usually issued by the State Department. This certificate proves the authenticity of official documents/papers that can be used abroad.

10. In NYS, who commissions a notary public?

a. County clerk

b. Licensing office

c. Secretary of State

d. Mayor

Answer C

It is the Secretary of State who commissions a notary public in NYS.

11. Which of the following is a false statement about a notary public and law?

a. A notary public should not ask for referrals from a lawyer

b. The notary public should not split fees with a lawyer

c. The notary public should not advertise that he can practice law when not qualified

d. A notary public should only give opinions on legal matters

Answer D

The rule is simple; a notary public should not only refrain from practicing law but should not give advice or opinions on legal matters.

12. From the initial application fee for a notary public, how much does the Secretary of State send to the County clerk?

a. $10

b. $20

c. $30

d. $40

Answer B

The Secretary of State usually sends $20 to the county clerk with the commission, the oath of office, and the official signature.

13. Where does the notary public usually stamp the Statement of Authority?

a. At the top of the instrument

b. Below the notary signature

c. Above the notary signature

d. At the end of the first page

Answer B

The Statement of authority is usually stamped just below the notary public signature.

14. If a notary public gets married and wants a name change, what fee will she be required to pay?

a. $2

b. $5

c. $7

d. $10

Answer D

A name change fee is $10, but if the name change is done at the time of renewal, there is no additional fee.

15. Recently your colleague at work has requested you notarize an affidavit. You should

a. Refuse as you know him personally

b. Administer an oath and complete the jurat

c. Ask for at least two pieces of govt issued photo IDs

d. Charge him $20

Answer B

Before notarizing an affidavit, it is important to administer an oath and complete the jurat.

16. Where are you most likely to find the following words, "Sworn to before me this _____ day of _____"?

a. Jurat

b. Oath

c. Confirmation

d. Affirmation

Answer A

The words, "Sworn to before me this _____ day of _____" are found in the jurat.

17. How long does the notary commission remain valid in New York?

a. One-year

b. Two years

c. Three years

d. Four years

Answer D

The term of the commission is valid for four years.

18. To practice as a notary in New York state, which of the following requirements must be met?

a. Have a notary bond

b. Have notary seal

c. Maintain a notary journal

d. Must be at least 18 years of age

Answer D

The applicant must be at least 18 years of age to apply for a notary public.

19. Which of the following is not a requirement for the commission process in New York?

a. Candidate must be at least 18 years of age

b. Candidate should have the equivalent of a common school education

c. Have completed an approved study course before the

test

d. Be free of any crimes

Answer C

New York candidates who want to become notaries do not have to take any type of approved course prior to the test.

20. What does it mean when an individual has an apostille?

a. He can use it instead of a passport to travel

b. He or she has a prior criminal conviction

c. He has access to the safe deposit box in the bank

d. He has certified documents for international use

Answer D

An apostille refers to a specialized certificate that is usually issued by the foreign ministry or consular service.

The apostille confirms that the documents have been obtained in a legal manner- allowing them to be recognized in other nations.

21. When a bank employee opens a safe deposit box that has passed its expiration date, what other person must be present at the same time?

a. The bank manager

b. The safe deposit box owner

c. A law enforcement office

d. A notary public

Answer D

When a safe deposit box has its lease expired, it needs to be opened up after the owner has been sent a letter. However, when a bank employee opens the safe deposit box, a notary public must be present to take the inventory and document the events.

22. Which word is often used interchangeably with deponent?

a. Defendant

b. Plaintiff

c. Affiant

d. Executor

Answer C

Deponent is often used interchangeably with affiant.

Made in United States
Orlando, FL
03 July 2023

34730942R00157